CARPENTRY WORKSHOP PRACTICE

CARPENTRY
WORKSHOP PRACTICE

BY

CHARLES F. MITCHELL, M.S.A.

[Lecturer on Carpentry and Joinery]

POLYTECHNIC INSTITUTE, 309 REGENT STREET, W.

AND

GEORGE A. MITCHELL, A.R.I.B.A.

[National Silver Medallist]

POLYTECHNIC INSTITUTE, 309 REGENT STREET, W.

PROFUSELY ILLUSTRATED

Woodworking

Woodworking is the process of making items from wood. Along with stone, mud and animal parts, wood was one of the first materials worked by early humans. There are incredibly early examples of woodwork, evidenced in Mousterian stone tools used by Neanderthal man, which demonstrate our affinity with the wooden medium. In fact, the very development of civilisation is linked to the advancement of increasingly greater degrees of skill in working with these materials.

Examples of Bronze Age wood-carving include tree trunks worked into coffins from northern Germany and Denmark and wooden folding-chairs. The site of Fellbach-Schmieden in Germany has provided fine examples of wooden animal statues from the Iron Age. Woodworking is depicted in many ancient Egyptian drawings, and a considerable amount of ancient Egyptian furniture (such as stools, chairs, tables, beds, chests) has been preserved in tombs. The inner coffins found in the tombs were also made of wood. The metal used by the Egyptians for woodworking tools was originally copper and eventually, after 2000 BC, bronze - as ironworking was unknown until much later. Historically, woodworkers relied upon the woods native to their region, until transportation and trade innovations made more exotic woods available to the craftsman.

Today, often as a contemporary artistic and 'craft' medium, wood is used both in traditional and modern styles; an excellent material for delicate as well as forceful artworks. Wood is used in forms of sculpture, trade, and decoration including chip carving, wood burning, and marquetry, offering a fascination, beauty, and complexity in the grain that often shows even when the medium is painted. It is in some ways easier to shape than harder substances, but an artist or craftsman must develop specific skills to carve it properly. 'Wood carving' is really an entire genre itself, and involves cutting wood generally with a knife in one hand, or a chisel by two hands - or, with one hand on a chisel and one hand on a mallet. The phrase may also refer to the finished product, from individual sculptures to hand-worked mouldings composing part of a tracery.

The making of sculpture in wood has been extremely widely practiced but survives much less well than the other main materials such as stone and bronze, as it is vulnerable to decay, insect damage, and fire. It therefore forms an important hidden element in the arts and crafts history of many cultures. Outdoor wood sculptures do not last long in most parts of the world, so we have little idea how the totem pole tradition developed. Many of the most important sculptures of China and Japan in particular are in wood, and the great majority of African sculptures and that of Oceania also use this medium. There are various forms of carving which can be utilised; 'chip carving' (a style of carving in which knives or chisels are used to remove small chips of the material), 'relief carving' (where figures are carved in a flat panel of wood), 'Scandinavian flat-plane' (where figures are carved in large flat planes, created primarily using a carving knife - and rarely rounded or sanded afterwards) and 'whittling' (simply carving shapes using just a knife). Each of these techniques will need slightly varying tools, but broadly speaking, a specialised 'carving knife' is essential, alongside a 'gouge' (a tool with a curved cutting edge used in a variety of forms and sizes for carving hollows, rounds and sweeping curves), a 'chisel' and a 'coping saw' (a small saw, used to cut off chunks of wood at once).

Wood turning is another common form of woodworking, used to create wooden objects on a lathe. Woodturning differs from most other forms of woodworking in that the wood is moving while a stationary tool is used to cut and shape it. There are two distinct methods of turning wood: 'spindle turning' and 'bowl' or 'faceplate turning'. Their key difference is in the orientation of the wood grain, relative to the axis of the lathe. This variation in orientation changes the tools and techniques used. In spindle turning, the grain runs lengthways along the lathe bed, as if a log was mounted in the lathe. Grain is thus always perpendicular to the direction of rotation under the tool. In bowl turning, the grain runs at right angles to the axis, as if a plank were mounted across the chuck. When a bowl blank rotates, the angle that the grain makes with the cutting tool continually changes between the easy cuts of lengthways and downwards across the grain to two places per rotation where the tool is cutting across the grain and even upwards across it. This varying grain angle limits some of the tools that may be used and requires additional skill in order to cope with it.

The origin of woodturning dates to around 1300 BC when the Egyptians first developed a two-person lathe. One person would turn the wood with a rope while the other used a sharp tool to cut shapes in the wood. The Romans improved the Egyptian design with the addition of a turning bow. Early bow lathes were also developed and used in Germany, France and Britain. In the Middle Ages a pedal replaced hand-operated turning, freeing both the craftsman's hands to hold the woodturning tools. The pedal was usually connected to a pole, often a straight-grained sapling. The system today is called the 'spring pole' lathe. Alternatively, a two-person lathe, called a 'great lathe', allowed a piece to turn continuously (like today's power lathes). A master would cut the wood while an apprentice turned the crank.

As an interesting aside, the term 'bodger' stems from pole lathe turners who used to make chair legs and spindles. A bodger would typically purchase all the trees on a plot of land, set up camp on the plot, and then fell the trees and turn the wood. The spindles and legs that were produced were sold in bulk, for pence per dozen. The bodger's job was considered unfinished because he only made component parts. The term now describes a person who leaves a job unfinished, or does it badly. This could not be more different from perceptions of modern carpentry; a highly skilled trade in which work involves the construction of buildings, ships, timber bridges and concrete framework. The word 'carpenter' is the English rendering of the Old French word *carpentier* (later, *charpentier*) which is derived from the Latin *carpentrius;* '(maker) of a carriage.' Carpenters traditionally worked with natural wood and did the rougher work such as framing, but today many other materials are also used and sometimes the finer trades of cabinet-making and furniture building are considered carpentry.

As is evident from this brief historical and practical overview of woodwork, it is an incredibly varied and exciting genre of arts and crafts; an ancient tradition still relevant in the modern day. Woodworkers range from hobbyists, individuals operating from the home environment, to artisan professionals with specialist workshops, and eventually large-scale factory operations. We hope the reader is inspired by this book to create some woodwork of their own.

PREFACE

THIS work has been prepared for those students, apprentices, mechanics, and others who are following a course of training in woodwork. It is hoped that the treatise will be found useful to those who are following the courses indicated by the Board of Education or that of the City and Guilds of London Institute, and especially to the still greater field of students who may not have the opportunity or privilege of attending a course of organised instruction.

In this book attention is called to timbers in general use, fastenings and tools used in ordinary practice, the common operations and processes necessary in the manipulation of wood, types of the various joints, and a few exercises of complete pieces of work, the acquirement of which knowledge will be found invaluable to all woodworkers.

The long experience in teaching, the many important successes in training students to achieve the highest honours obtainable in Carpentry and Joinery, and the call for this, the Third Edition of this work, suggests the hope that all who may have the opportunity of taking this course of instruction in the use of tools employed in the handicrafts using wood, may find it to be a good educational discipline in training the hand and eye to accuracy, and that the practical knowledge of the working of the most applicable and sympathetic of all materials will develop, stimulate, and make useful the mental and observant faculties of all who may be sufficiently patient and privileged to undergo this necessary training of a modern liberal education.

CHARLES F. MITCHELL.

Polytechnic Technical School,
  309, Regent Street, W.

CONTENTS

SYLLABUS OF THE BOARD OF EDUCATION, August 1st, 1904

MANUAL INSTRUCTION IN WOOD

(1) Woodwork

ALL lessons in woodwork should be associated with drawing. Each member of the class should, as a rule, make a measured working drawing (plan and elevation or isometric view) of each exercise before proceeding to the work at the bench, and must then work as far as possible from his own drawing, not from a diagram or model, which may only be used so far as necessary to elucidate the drawing. The pupils should be practised in orthographic and isometric or conventional representations of simple constructions ; these should be to scale and dimensioned, but an isometric scale need not be used. Drawing to scale from sketches on the blackboard is a good exercise, but students should not, except in the earliest lessons, be allowed to copy any drawing exactly as it is placed before them ; they should generally be required to transpose from orthographic into isometric projection or *vice versâ*, and to draw additional views frequently. The pupils may also make dimensioned freehand sketches (plans, elevations, etc.) of the objects they are about to make, from good models, before proceeding to make their own finished working drawing. Drawing-board, T-square, and set-squares should be used. The aim of the teacher, in all the exercises, should be to secure accuracy rather than quickness of work.

In connection with their practical exercises the

pupils should receive object-lessons on the nature of the different kinds of timber commonly used, and on the principles underlying the construction of the simpler tools.

The lessons should comprise such subjects as the following :—

1. **Timber.**—Its nature, growth, description, qualities, seasoning, uses, etc. Countries and ports from which we receive our supplies, the forms in which it is brought into the market.

Description of the more common kinds of woods, and purposes for which they are best adapted.

2. **Tools.**—Their names, proper uses, correct handling, principles of construction, and the modes of hardening, sharpening, and using them.

The varieties and uses of the various accessories required in construction, such as nails, screws, glue.

The bench work should take the form of a series of carefully graduated exercises, each successive exercise introducing a new tool or a new mode of using one with which the class are already acquainted. The common tendency to allow the work to take the form of amateur " Carpentry," and that too often of a rough character, should be carefully guarded against. It should always be remembered that the object of the instruction is to train the hand and eye by accurate measurement and by the use of tools, and to impart a knowledge of the principles of simple construction ; also that a high degree of skill and rapidity of execution, which are essential to the artisan and are generally obtained by the frequent repetition of the same exercise, are not to be aimed at. The production of a large number of articles should, similarly, not be made an object of chief concern, especially where this would involve the frequent repetition of the same exercise, or roughness of finish.

The exercises should be selected so as to give variety, and should involve practice in the varied use

of different tools and in different methods of construction.

The pupils may be exercised at first in sawing
out from a plank pieces of wood of such dimensions
as may be conveniently used in future exercises,
the pieces so sawn to be cut across in suitable lengths
and planed true to required sizes.

The exercises should include making models of
the ordinary carpentry joints, such as a simple cross-
halving joint, a dovetail halving joint, a mortise and
tenon joint, a slip tenon and simple bridle joint.
These should be followed by exercises in making
simple frames having three or more joints.

Subsequently the pupils may also well be exercised in making models of some useful object, such
as a box with dovetail joint, a knife-cleaning box, a
corner bracket.

With pupils who have made some progress, exercises in hard wood might be practised, such as making
a mitre box, a T-square 18 inches long, a wooden
try square 12 inches long.

For most of the exercises, American yellow pine,
or best yellow deal, may be used. For the hard wood
exercises, American bass wood, beech, or pear wood.

SCHEME OF INSTRUCTION

First Year's Course

Exercises in Joint Work.—Housing joint, cross
halving joint, T halving joint, notched T-joint, notched
cross joint.

Models.—Window wedge, plant label, square
prism, square flower stick, key label, flat ruler,
string winder, round ruler, flower pot ·cross.

Tools used.—Rip and tenon saws, jack and
smoothing planes, firmer chisel, compass, rule, gauge,
hammer, brace and bit, try square.

Second Year's Course

Exercises in Joint Work.—Mortise and tenon joint, bridle joint, tongue and groove joint.

Models.—Bench hook, pen tray, flower pot stand, flat ruler, nailed box, finger plate, bracket, set squares.

New Tools Introduced. — Rebate plane, trying plane, mortise gauge, mitre square gauge, nails and screws, glue.

Third Year's Course

Exercises in Joint Work.—Cogging joint, mortise bridle joint, oblique halving joints, Tredgold's notched halving joints. Common box dove-tailing.

Models.—T-square, try square, towel roller and rests, drawing board, soap-box, scoop, mirror frame, knife box, organ pipe and other examples of science apparatus.

New Tools. — Spokeshave, bevel, dovetail saw, cutting gauge.

CARPENTRY
WORKSHOP PRACTICE

TIMBER

BOTANISTS classify plants under two heads, the Phanerogams and Cryptogams, the flowering and the non-flowering plants.

The trees from which timber for use in construction

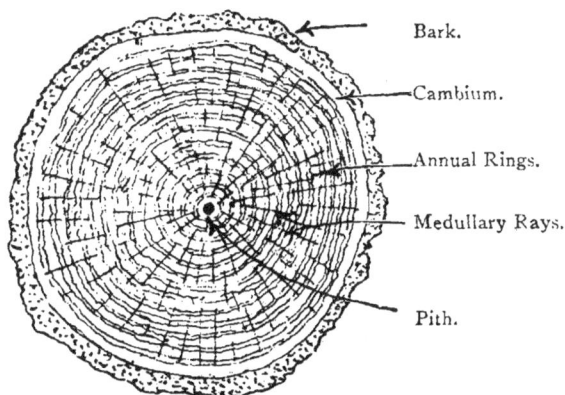

Bark.

Cambium.

Annual Rings.

Medullary Rays.

Pith.

FIG. I.

and for furniture, etc., is obtained, are of the former division. Generally the timber known as soft wood is from the coniferous order, or needle leaf Phanerogams ; whilst those known as hard woods are mainly of the non-coniferous order, or the broad leaf type. The Phanerogams are subdivided into two classes : the exogens or outward growers, and the endogens or inward growers.

The exogens comprise those trees which increase

in bulk by successive accretions in concentric layers of the substance of which the tree is formed on the outside of the pith, or of the preceding layers, and directly beneath the bark or skin.

If a transverse section be taken through the stem of a typical exogen such as the oak, as shown in Fig. 1, upon examination the following parts will be seen :—

1. Pith.
2. Annual Rings.
3. Medullary Rays.
4. Cambium.
5. Bark.

Pith.—The pith, which is the first formed portion of the tree, consists of cellular tissue, and in the young plant the functions of vegetation are carried on through it ; but after a few years, the circulation of the sap takes place through the annual rings which have been deposited, the pith then ceasing to perform any active part in the life of the tree, and in course of time decays.

Annual Rings.—The annual rings consist of cellular tissue and woody fibre deposited in concentric cylinders about the pith.   The term annual is applied to them, because, in temperate climates, one layer is deposited yearly ; but in the tropics, where the seasons are not so distinctly marked, there may be more than one layer per annum.

The annual rings consist of two parts—the spring and the autumn wood.   These portions are respectively formed during the rising and descending of the sap by the activity of the cambium cells, these latter consisting of a layer of generative tissue immediately adjacent to the bark, and having the characteristic property of dividing and multiplying under the action of heat and moisture, forming the annual rings and also the new material for the bark.   The cells formed during the autumn are smaller in section and more compact than those formed during the spring, and accordingly are easily observable in the wood, their greater density causing them to appear darker than in the spring wood.

Medullary Rays.—These are thin bands of cellular tissue extending in a horizontal direction and showing as lines in a cross section of the tree, and radiating from the pith interposed between the woody fibres. Their function is to act as a duct to allow of the transmission of moisture and sap to the interior of the tree.

Bark.—The bark is the outer covering of trees, formed of woody fibres. As spring-time approaches the ascending sap causes the bark to become loose, and the latter, being slightly elastic, stretches under the centrifugal action of the newly formed zone. As the tree increases in age the continuous addition of annual layers causes the outer layers of the bark to split and portions to break away and fall.

Felling.—Trees should not be felled before they have reached maturity, a period the experienced forester can determine from the appearance of the foliage, the size and other indications peculiar to different woods and varying conditions.

If the tree is felled before it has matured, the timber will not be durable ; if felled very much after, it will be brittle and inelastic. The proper season for felling the tree is mid-winter, because at that time vegetation is practically at a standstill, and the newly formed cells are in a better condition to resist decomposition than at any previous stage in their formation ; if felled while the cambium is active, and the sap is circulating, the partly formed cells rapidly decompose, and are liable to induce decay in the otherwise sound portions of the tree. There is also much less moisture in the tree at mid-winter than at any other period of the year.

Conversion.—Immediately the tree has been felled, the log should be trimmed of its branches, barked, and sawn to dimensions suitable for the final purposes for which the wood is intended.

The timber is cut lengthwise in a direction either :—
1st, tangentially to, or as a chord of, the annual rings ;
or, 2nd, radially. The first method is employed in
highly figured timbers, to obtain the effect of the
obliquely cut annual rings, also in soft woods to obtain
the maximum quantity of timber of rectangular
section ; the second method is adopted to obtain
the effect of the medullary rays, and is extensively
applied to oak.

Seasoning.—After the wood is converted, it is
stacked to season, the object of which is to dry the
free moisture out of the timber. There are two
methods in common practice for accomplishing this.
The first, known as natural seasoning ; the second,
the desiccating process. The first method consists
in stacking the stuff in the open and preventing any
damage from the effects of the sun or the rain by
covering the top with a roof, or, preferably, stacking
in a shed which is open at the sides.

Secondly, the principle of the desiccating process
is to stack the stuff in a heated chamber to accelerate
the drying out of the moisture ; it is more applicable
to small scantlings, and is usually adopted in large
firms to work that has been partially prepared. The
stuff, having been first seasoned naturally and sawn
to scantling and planed, is placed in heated chambers
to dry out any excess of moisture it may still contain.

With both methods great care should be exercised
to stack the unseasoned stuff perfectly true and out
of winding ; and that arrangement is to be preferred
which allows a current of air to pass over the greatest
area of the surface of the stuff.

Selection.—In selecting timber, the following
points should be noted. The timber should be of a
bright appearance, dulness in almost all examples
betokening decay.

In sawing, the timber should cut short, and not
clog the teeth of the saw ; and in planing it should

finish with a silky lustre. The timber should have its characteristic odour, any deviation from this generally denoting decay. There should not be an excess of sap-wood, as this must on no account be used. The stuff should be free from shakes, of which there are three well-known varieties—viz. heart shake, star shake, and cup shake. The first originates at the pith, and radiates in a number of clefts from the centre ; this is generally due to the decay and drying of the central portion of the tree. The second is the star shake. The clefts in this case commence at the outside, radiating inwards, and may be the result of decay and the drying of the outer portion of the tree, or to unequal or violent expansion and contraction due to sudden changes of temperature, or to the freezing of the moisture in the outer portion of the tree.

The third is the cup shake, which consists of the separation of the annual rings from each other. Where this occurs near the exterior, it may be due to the expansion of the outer layers during hard frosts, and, if occurring near the centre, to the shearing stress set up in the tree in bending when the latter is subjected to high winds or to violent gusts. The other kinds of shakes, and combinations of the three above mentioned, may be due to the destructive agency of the wind, as they are found to be very prevalent in trees grown in exposed positions.

Wandering heart and twisted fibres are defects most probably due to a prevalent wind, which has caused the tree to tend to turn constantly in one direction ; such timber is practically useless for constructional purposes, as so many of the fibres are cut during conversion. The timber should be uniform in colour, any sudden changes of colour other than the difference between the heart and sap-wood, such as white or red patches or spots, being usually attributed to some form of decay. The annual rings

B

should be close and uniform ; timbers in which the rings are large, or not uniform, are usually weak.

Shrinkage of Timber.—The medullary rays are thin, hard, vertical plates of cellular tissue, in harder woods especially, practically unyielding and unshrinkable. The seasoned section of a piece of timber may be determined by imagining these plates to act as ribs of a system (such as a fan) and closing upon its centre.

Decay in Timber.—Decay usually commences with the decomposition of the albuminous substances contained in the timber. The two forms of decay most generally known are the dry rot and the wet rot. The former is a chemical decomposition caused by an external vegetable organism in an imperfectly ventilated atmosphere ; while the latter is a chemical decomposition of the sap and fibre of unseasoned wood, or, if seasoned, results from exposure to the moisture of a temperate atmosphere.

Dry Rot is caused by the growth of fungi, the spores of which, floating about in the atmosphere, alight on timber, and if conditions are favourable, germinate and insert their roots into the timber, the constituents of which they decompose, and so obtain their nutriment. These plants rapidly spread over the whole of the timber, and attack other timbers in the vicinity, causing them to crumble. The conditions favourable for dry rot are a warm, humid atmosphere, insufficient ventilation, and the presence of any green sap in the timber. All stuff in constructional works should therefore be thoroughly seasoned before being used, and well ventilated when fixed.

Wet Rot is caused by the oxidation of lignin and other substances in the presence of air and water, the oxygen combining with the carbon to form CO_2, and with the hydrogen to form H_2O. The hydrogen, however, becomes more rapidly oxidised than the carbon ; consequently, the latter remains in excess and a brown snuff-coloured powder results, which has a larger proportion of carbon than the woody fibre.

Moisture is necessary to the process, which takes place in the open air, 60° Fahr. being the most favourable temperature.

In trees which have passed their maturity the decay usually commences with the pith, hence the necessity of cutting through and thoroughly examining the heart of large timbers.

The timbers in use for constructional and general work are classified under two heads—1st, soft woods from the needle-leaf or cone-bearing trees ; 2nd, hard woods from the broad-leaf trees.

SOFT WOODS.—The first section known as soft woods includes the pines and spruce, as follows :—

Northern Pine (Pinus sylvestris).—This timber is obtained largely from the following ports : Memel, Dantzic, and Stettin in Prussia ; St. Petersburg, Riga, Onega, Archangel, and Narva in Russia ; Christiania and Dram in Norway; Gefle and Soderham in Sweden. It is also extensively grown in Great Britain, being known here as Scotch fir. It is of a light yellow colour ; the annual rings are clearly defined, consisting of a light and a dark portion ; they are regular and about $\frac{3}{16}$ inch in thickness ; medullary rays not visible ; straight grained ; weighs about 36 pounds per cubic foot ; contains resinous substances which render it durable ; it is strong and elastic ; does not warp nor shake to any extent ; is easy to work, and cuts clean and short. This wood is largely used for constructional work and for joinery, being suitable both for internal and external work.

American Yellow or White Pine (Pinus strobus).— This timber is exported from Quebec, St. John's, and Shedac, and a few other Canadian ports. It is sometimes known as Weymouth pine. It is of a whitish or pale yellow colour, annual rings not very distinct ; they are regular, and about $\frac{1}{4}$ inch in thickness ; medullary rays not visible ; it is very straight grained ; weighs about 29 pounds per cubic foot ; is not as strong nor elastic as northern pine ; does not warp much, but is liable to shake ; is very easy to work, and is used chiefly in joinery work for mouldings and wide panels ; it does not prove durable when used externally.

Pitch Pine (Pinus rigida).—This timber grows in the south-eastern States of North America, and is shipped chiefly from the ports of Savannah and Pensacola. It is of a dark yellow or light reddish-brown tint ; annual rings clearly defined and of a uniform width of about $\frac{3}{16}$ inch ; medullary rays not visible ; it is straight grained, and can be obtained in great lengths ; is highly charged with resinous substances, rendering it very durable ; weighs about 46 pounds per cubic foot ; it is very strong and, compared with other pines, difficult to work ; has a tendency to stick to the tools on account of its large quantity of resin. It is subject to heart and cup shake, shrinks considerably in drying, and also tends to warp.

The straightness of its grain, great strength, and the large scantlings obtainable render it valuable for constructional work ; it is largely used for ornamental joinery work on account of the beautiful figure of its grain, although its excessive shrinkage renders it unsuitable for this purpose.

White Fir or Spruce (Abies excelsa).—This wood is obtained chiefly from the following ports : Onega, Narva, and St. Petersburg in Russia ; Christiania, Dram, and Frederikstadt in Norway ; and Gottenburg, Sandsvall, and Hernosand in Sweden. It is of a whitish or very pale yellow colour ; annual rings clearly defined, uniform, and about $\frac{3}{16}$ inch in thickness ; medullary rays not visible. The wood is usually straight grained, weighs about 32 pounds per cubic foot, contains resinous substances, but not to the same extent as northern pine. It is strong and elastic ; it warps and splits in drying ; is tough, but easy to work when free from knots, which in this wood are very hard ; it cuts clean and free with the saw, finishes with a silky lustre from the plane, and is sufficiently close grained to take a polish. The best kinds of this wood are used largely for internal joinery work ; it is not durable when used externally ; the coarser varieties are used for packing-cases, and for similar rough purposes. It has a beautiful figure, and is often varnished in order to obtain the maximum effect. It is much used for constructional work, but is neither as strong nor as durable as northern pine.

Larch (Làrix europœa), Europe, Great Britain.— Colour, light yellow or brownish white, straight in grain and free from knots, tough, very durable and strong, works up well. Weighs about 40 pounds per cubic foot. Much used for sleepers, scaffold poles, piles, and fencing.

Cedar (Cedrus Libani).—Cedar is a name given to many trees resembling in their characteristics the true cedar, which is a native of Lebanon and South West Asia. It was introduced into England in the latter half of the seventeenth century. Cedar belongs to the coniferous order. It is reddish-brown in colour, straight, and open grained, easily worked. It has a strong but not unpleasant odour, very obnoxious to insects, and is therefore used much for the internal parts of cabinets. Most of the cedar in use in this country is the Cedrela odorata, and is brought from Cuba, Trinidad, and Honduras. Its weight is about 28 pounds per cubic foot.

Kauri Pine (Agathis Australis), North Island, New Zealand.—Whitish yellow to light brown in colour, straight grained, free from knots, close grained, firm, strong, and elastic, easily worked, finishing with a silky lustre, takes a good polish ; weighs $37\frac{1}{2}$ pounds per cubic foot ; very durable ; useful for all kinds of joinery work. Can be obtained in great widths.

Sequoia (Sequoia sempervirens), California.—Of brownish-red colour, straight grained, light, soft, and not strong, easily worked. Used for cabinet work and internal joinery work.

HARD WOODS.—The second section, known as hard woods, includes oak, mahogany, etc.

Oak (Quercus).—This timber abounds in Europe (including Great Britain), Asia, and America. There are a great many species of oak, but all have the same general characteristics, differing only in minor details.

There are two kinds native to this country—viz. Q. pedunculata and Q. sessiliflora ; the chief difference between the two lies in the arrangement of the flowers and leaves.

The former is generally supposed to be the more durable ; the latter is credited with being tougher and more difficult to rend, and can be obtained in greater lengths, and is straighter grained than the pedunculata ; it is light brown in colour ; annual rings distinct and generally fairly uniform, about ⅛ inch in thickness ; medullary rays strongly marked ; grain fairly straight, but in trees grown in the open usually gnarled and twisted ; weighs about 48 pounds per cubic foot. It contains gallic acid, which rapidly corrodes ironwork, thus preventing the general employment of these two materials together ; it is subject to warping and shaking ; is very tough and difficult to work, but will take a high finish. It is greatly prized for ornamental joinery work on account of its figure and the beautiful markings of the medullary rays when the log is cut lengthwise radially ; it is very durable and strong, and therefore valuable for heavy constructional work ; it is very lasting in either a wet or a dry situation, and proves more durable than most other woods in an alternately wet and dry position.

Mahogany (Swietenia mahagoni).—Mahogany is obtained from the West Indies and Central America, the chief supplies coming from Cuba and Honduras.

Mahogany is of a reddish-brown colour ; annual rings not very distinct but uniform ; medullary rays invisible ; fairly straight grained, weight (Cuba) about 53 pounds per cubic foot, (Honduras) about 35 pounds per cubic foot. It is strong, but inclined to be brittle ; it warps, shrinks, and shakes very little ; it is hard, not very difficult to work, and is capable of receiving a high finish and a splendid polish.

The wood lasts well when used internally, but is not durable when employed for external purposes ; it is chiefly used for cabinet work and ornamental joinery, for shop fittings and internal finishings. Cuba or Spanish mahogany, as it is sometimes called, is darker and richer in colour than the Honduras, and has a more wavy grain than the latter, and produces when cut a beautiful figure ; this renders it very durable for the highest class of joinery work. It is harder and denser, but does not attain such large dimensions as the Honduras. The Cuba may be easily distinguished from the Honduras by a chalk-like substance filling its pores. The Honduras is chiefly noted for the straightness of its grain, rendering it particularly adaptable for sticking mouldings. It is used for all kinds of internal joinery and cabinet work ; is largely used for pattern-making on account of the small amount of its shrinkage ; it is sometimes known as bay-mahogany or bay-wood.

Elm (Ulmus).—This timber is grown in large quantities in England. It is of a brown colour ; annual rings distinct ; medullary rays invisible to the eye ; has a very twisted grain ; weighs 37 pounds per cubic foot ; it is very liable to warp and shake ; is very tough and difficult to work ; it is very durable when kept either thoroughly wet or perfectly dry. It is used chiefly for the sides and bottoms of carts, the hubs of wheels, for coffins, wood pulley-blocks, and for all similar purposes requiring a tough, strong wood.

Ash (Fraxinus).—This timber is obtained in large

quantities in Great Britain. It is of a light brown colour ; annual rings distinct ; medullary rays not visible ; is straight grained ; weighs 52 pounds per cubic foot, and is very tough, strong, and elastic ; is subject to shake in seasoning ; durable if properly seasoned ; has a large proportion of sap-wood. Its great elasticity debars its use for all large structural operations, but it is valuable as shafts for hammers, spokes for wheels, for oars, and in any position where it will be subjected to sudden stresses.

Beech (Fagus).—Large quantities of beech are obtained in England. It is of a light reddish-brown colour ; annual rings distinct ; medullary rays strongly marked ; can be obtained in great lengths and is very straight grained ; weighs 43 pounds per cubic foot ; is strong, tough, and durable if kept dry ; is close grained and easy to work, and will take a high finish. It is largely used for furniture, and owing to its close and even grain is valuable for tools which require an even wearing surface.

Plane (Platanus orientalis), Levant and Asia Minor.—Cultivated in Great Britain. Light yellow colour, slight reddish tinge ; close grained, easily worked ; weight average 43 pounds per cubic foot. Used for cabinet work, turnery, etc. Plane trees chiefly cultivated in England for ornamental purposes. A similar wood (Platanus occidentalis) is obtained from North America.

Sycamore (Acer pseudo-platanus). — This timber abounds in England. This wood is sometimes known as the common or great maple. It is brownish- or yellowish-white in colour ; annual rings distinct ; medullary rays small but distinct, often has a beautiful figure ; fairly strong, fairly difficult to work ; weighs about 38 pounds per cubic foot, is durable when kept dry. It is used chiefly for furniture and ornamental joinery.

Maple (Acer campestre), supplied from England,

Europe, Asia, and America. The European variety is light brown in colour. Annual rings distinct, slightly wavy. Medullary rays fine, indistinct in longitudinal sections. Fine grained, finishes with satin-like lustre, takes a high polish, frequently curled or speckled, then termed Birds Eye Maple. Weight, 52 pounds per cubic foot. Much used by cabinet makers, especially for veneers.

Rock Maple (Acer campestre), North America.— Colour, white with reddish tinge ; annual rings distinct ; close grained, wavy, compact, and tough ; finishes with a silky lustre, takes a high polish ; weighs 43 pounds per cubic foot. Much used for furniture, joinery, stairs, doors, etc. Is eminently fire-resisting, and is used to comply with the London County Council fire regulations. It does not readily splinter, and is largely used for the floors of skating rinks.

Pear Wood (Pyrus communis), Europe.—Light brown colour, with pinkish tinge, fairly hard, close grained, tough, easily cut in any direction, annual rings not very distinct. Much used for cabinet work, turnery, tee, and set squares and other similar purposes.

Basswood (Tilia americana). — This wood is obtained from the United States and Canada. It is of a yellowish-white colour ; annual rings indistinct ; medullary rays invisible ; is straight grained and of a uniform substance, soft and easy to work, may be cut easily across or in any direction of the grain, and can be obtained in widths up to 2 feet 6 inches. It is largely used for furniture and piano work, and weighs about 28 pounds per cubic foot.

Lime (Tilia europœa). — Obtained plentifully in England. It is of a whitish colour ; annual rings distinct ; medullary rays invisible ; very straight grained and of uniform density, very soft and easy to work in any direction. It is used for cabinet work and fine carvings, and weighs about 33 pounds per cubic foot.

Walnut (Juglans regia), Britain and Europe.—Dark

brown colour, with dark wavy grain; fairly difficult to work; takes a high finish and polish. Weighs about 44 pounds per cubic foot. Walnut burrs have a beautifully mottled appearance, and the wood is much valued for veneers. The ordinary wood is used largely for ornamental joinery, cabinet work, and for gun stocks. Walnut from Italy is generally the best, and next in order the Austrian, then the French, and lastly the English.

Walnut (Juglans Nigra).—From Eastern North America.—Dark brown colour with a purplish tinge, hard, tough, and strong, straighter in grain than the European wood; weighs about 57 pounds per cubic foot; can be worked up to a high finish, and takes a good polish. Chiefly used for ornamental joinery and cabinet work, and also for gunstocks.

Walnut (Juglans alba), North America.—Lighter in colour and straighter in grain than the previous, very tough, durable, and strong. Weighs about 51 pounds per cubic foot. Largely used for furniture of an inferior quality.

Satin Walnut (Liquidambar styraciflua), Eastern United States.—Colour, light reddish-brown, strongly marked figure, close grained, soft, and fairly tough; can be highly finished, and receives a good polish. Weighs about 37 pounds per cubic foot. Largely used for furniture of an inferior quality.

Butternut (Juglans cinerea), Eastern North America —Reddish-brown in colour, coarser in grain, lighter in weight, and not so durable as ordinary walnut. Used for inferior work in cabinet making.

Teak (Tectona grandis), Central and Southern India, Burmah.—Rich brown colour, straight and close grained, easily worked, takes a high finish and good polish, contains an aromatic oil which endows the timber with great durability and preserves any ironwork in connection, contains a phosphate of lime secretion that soon takes the edge from cutting tools;

it is very durable and strong, does not warp nor shrink much when once seasoned, weighs about 49 pounds per cubic foot. Teak is much used for shipbuilding, joinery, and cabinet work.

Jarrah (Eucalyptus marginata), South-western Australia.—Red colour, similar in appearance to mahogany, with a beautiful figure, close and straight grained, hard, and durable ; can be worked up to a high finish, and takes a good polish. Weight variable, between 55 and 75 pounds per cubic foot. Owing to its tendency to warp and shrink it is unreliable for joinery or large furniture, but for small work has been much used, being very durable and hard ; it is especially suitable for wood paving, and is much used for that purpose, also for sleepers, piles, etc.

Padouk (Pterocarpus indicus), Burmah, Southern China, Philippines.—Dark red colour, wavy grain, similar in appearance to mahogany, close but coarse grain, hard, works well, takes a high polish ; weighs 60 pounds per cubic foot. Used for joinery and furniture.

Sabicu (Lysiloma sabicu), West Indies, Cuba.— Dark brown colour, close grained, dense and hard, strong and elastic, some varieties highly figured, can be worked to a fine finish, takes a good polish ; weighs about 60 pounds per cubic foot. Much used in shipbuilding and furniture.

Amboyna (Pterocarpus indicus), obtained from the Moluccas and New Guinea.—Light reddish-brown colour, hard, and of a mottled and curly grain, takes a beautiful polish. Used for inlaying. Sold by weight.

Box (Buxus sempervirens), Western Asia, Southern Europe, and Northern Europe.—Light yellow colour, annual rings indistinct, close grained and hard ; weighs from 70 to 80 pounds per cubic foot ; can be worked up to a fine finish, cuts smoothly in any direction. Much used for turning and inlay work, and also for the wood blocks for engraving purposes.

Ebony (Diospyros ebenum), obtained from Southern India and Ceylon.—Deep black colour, annual rings scarcely discernible, very fine grained; weighs 70 to 80 pounds per cubic foot, difficult to work, receives a high polish. Much used for furniture, veneer, and inlaid work.

Rosewood (Dalbergia nigra), South America.—Reddish-brown in colour, with black streaks, emits a pleasant odour, a beautiful grain, takes a high polish; weighs about 48 pounds per cubic foot. It is valued for all kinds of furniture, and is much used for veneers. There are a number of woods answering to the general description termed rosewoods. None of these have anything to do with the rose.

Sandal Wood (Santalum album), Southern India and Malay Archipelago.—Colour yellowish-brown; annual rings, close grained and hard. Much used for wood ornaments, cabinet work, and carving. It has a fragrant odour.

Tulip Wood (Liriodendron tulipefera), North America.—Light yellow or brownish colour, close and straight grained, easily worked, takes a good polish. Used for building in America, and for carriage building and cabinet making in England.

TulipWood (Physocalymnia scaberrunum), Brazil.—A beautiful reddish colour, with dark-red stripes. Much used for inlaying in cabinet work.

Satin Wood (Chloroxylon sweetenia), from Central and Southern India.—Light yellow or brown in colour, hard and close grained, with a feathery and mottled appearance; can be highly finished, and takes a good polish. It is largely used for cabinet work and for veneers. Woods similar in colour and characteristics to the above, termed satin woods, are also obtained from Australia, and in large quantities from the West Indies. The figure of the wood from the East Indies is in streaks, whilst that from the West presents a wavy appearance.

FASTENINGS

THE following fastenings are commonly used by the
wood worker :—Glue, wedges, keys, buttons, angle-
blocks, dowels, trenails, brads, nails, spikes, screws,
bolts, nuts and washers, dogs, iron straps, and sockets.

Glue.—This is procured from the horns, hoofs,
hides, and other parts of animals by steeping, washing,

FIG. 2.

boiling, straining, melting, reboiling, and casting into
cakes.

There are two varieties in general use—the Scotch
and the French ; the former is very adhesive, but
presents a black appearance ; the latter is not quite
as effective, but is lighter in colour.

The vessels for heating glue consist of an inner
and an outer pot, as shown in Fig. 2, the former
fitting into the latter, and being brought into contact

at their upper rim only. The outer pot, which is brought into contact with the gas jet or fire, is partly filled with water ; the inner pot, which contains the glue to be melted, when in position is partly immersed in the water in the outer pot ; this water, when boiling, supplies the necessary heat to dissolve the glue. This arrangement is adopted, as it is imperative that the glue should be dissolved by a wet heat.

It is important to note that glue deteriorates if exposed for a long time to a great heat, or if it be re-heated many times. More should not therefore be made than is required for one or two days' use ; and it should be softened by being well soaked in cold water before being heated, to reduce the time required to accomplish that operation.

The method of preparing glue is as follows :— The cakes are broken into small pieces and placed in a pail containing cold water, where they remain for about a day to soften ; they are then placed in the inner pot, and sufficient water is added to cover the same ; the glue-pot is then placed upon the heating apparatus and boiled gently for about two hours, during which time it should be frequently stirred to ensure uniformity ; at the end of this time it will be ready for use. Glue should be applied while hot, but must not be burnt. For joint-making, glue should be strained by running it while hot and fluid through a coarse canvas, which serves to retain any dirt or foreign matter.

Wedges are pieces of wood cut with two length faces parallel and with two faces inclined to and intersecting each other, but at right angles to the former pair. These are extensively used in wood-work to secure tenons in mortises and to fix parts together.

Keys is the name given to wedges (as shown in Fig. 142), generally of hard wood, used to pull parts together that may be required to be taken to pieces afterwards.

Buttons are small pieces of wood, tongued at one end, and fixed by a screw to a wide panel. The tongue of the button enters a groove in, or clips a batten at, right angles to the wide panel, the effect being to keep the panel secure to the batten, and yet leave the former free to expand or contract in one plane. This method is often employed for securing wide surfaces of wood, such as table tops (as shown in Figs. 202 and 204) or drawing-boards, to framing or battens.

Angle-Blocks.—Pieces of wood, triangular in section, generally of dry American yellow pine, with two length faces at right angles to each other ; they are often used to secure two adjacent parts together, such as the riser and step of a stair, by saturating the length faces at right angles to each other with glue and well rubbing the glue-covered surfaces of the angle-block against the adjacent faces of the two pieces required to be kept together.

Dowels are small, hard-wood pins, circular or polyhedral in section. When being prepared, to ensure continuity in the fibres, they must be rent and trimmed with a chisel, and not cut with a saw. Where desired to be circular in section they are first trimmed approximately so with the chisel, after which they are driven through a hole in an iron plate, the latter being provided with a number of holes of the exact size of the joiner's twist bits. Dowel pins are used for securing mortise and tenon joints (as shown in Fig. 85), and to keep boards that form wide surfaces in the same plane.

Trenails.—Hard-wood pins of large diameter are called trenails, and are extensively used in carpentry, or in positions where iron fastenings would be liable to rust.

Nails.—Nails are pieces of metal plate or wire, tapering or prismatical, with points, all of which are cast, cut, or stamped with heads. They may be obtained in cast-iron, wrought-iron, steel, zinc, copper, brass, or in composition metal. The greater number have one pair of sides parallel in length, which should always be driven in with those sides parallel to the length grain, to reduce the tendency of the nail to split the wood in its progress after each blow. Hard woods are bored to receive the nails; but in the softer woods this is not always necessary. There is a great variety of nails, those in common use being manufactured from wrought-iron or steel.

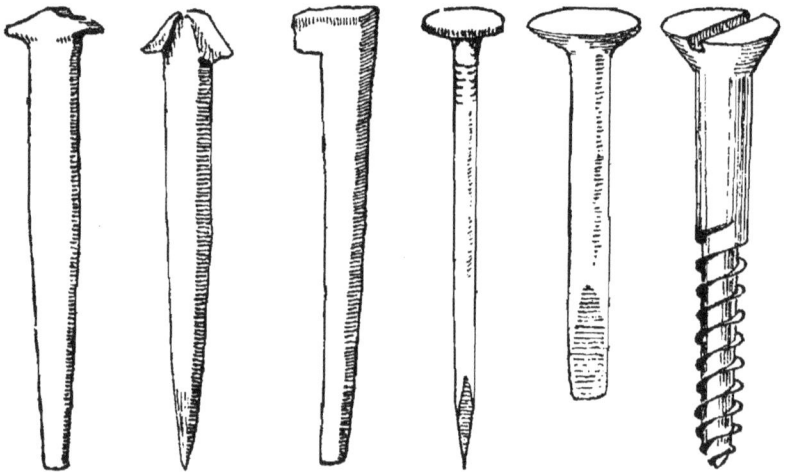

FIG. 3.   FIG. 4.   FIG. 5.   FIG. 6.   FIG. 7.   FIG. 8.

Cast-iron Nails.—These have been used for slating purposes, but are very brittle, and are now discarded.

Wrought-iron Nails.—Cut clasps are cut by machinery from wrought-iron plates, to the form shown in Fig. 3, and are the nails most commonly used. Clasp nails 4 inches and above in length are known as spikes. Nails cut from plates of wrought-iron by manual labour, of the form shown in Fig. 4, are particularly known as wrought nails, and possess the property of bending sufficiently to clinch without breaking. Of late years, however, these have been produced by machinery, which has been improved to cut sufficiently and yet not to destroy the tenacity and pliability of good wrought-iron.

Brads.—Tapering nails of parallel thickness with heads projecting only on one side, as shown in Fig. 5, are used to connect parts together where the nail hole is required to be of the minimum size.

Needle Points are small steel pins, circular in section, similar to the ordinary needle, but without eyes. These are used to fix hard wood moulding to joiners' work, and also in the process of veneering.

Veneering Pins are small, thin, steel pins without heads, used for the purpose of holding the veneer in its place until the caul is in position. When the glue is thoroughly set these pins are withdrawn.

Clout Nails.—These are nails with shanks rectangular or circular in section, with large, flat, circular heads, as shown in Fig. 7. Small, clout-headed nails are called tacks. Zinc, copper, and composition nails of this type are largely used to secure slating, as these resist oxidation better than the iron.

Wire Nails.—These are usually circular, elliptical, or rectangular in section, and are usually known as French nails. They are very tough and strong, and do not break so readily as the clasp, but whilst being driven in position are apt to split the wood. Those circular in section (as shown in Fig. 6) are often used in packing-case making, and the elliptical, with small heads, for securing mouldings to joiners' work.

Screws.—Fig. 8 shows the form of screw used for fixing woodwork. They are usually made of wrought-iron or of brass, the latter resisting oxidation better than the former metal. They are made with one end tapering to a point to permit of the screw entering more easily, the thread being of a coarse pitch. The shape of the head generally determines the name, such as round-headed, countersunk-headed, etc.

Bolts are large screws with square or hexagonal heads, and are extensively used for carpentry work.

c

Large timbers are often held together with bolts, passed through holes bored in the timbers and secured by nuts, which are square or hexagonal pieces of wrought-iron similar to the heads, but drilled and tapped to receive the shank of the bolt. The thread on these bolts and nuts is finer and of a less pitch than on the screws for wood.

Dogs are pieces of flat or round wrought-iron, bent at ends and pointed (as shown in Fig. 9).

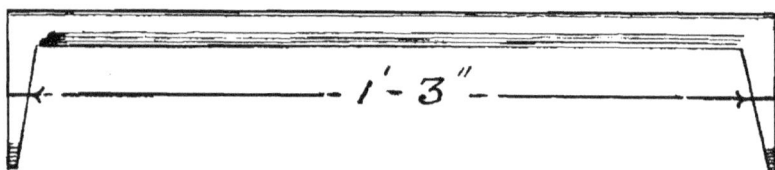

FIG. 9.

They are used in temporary carpentry work to secure large timbers which rest on or abut against each other, the pointed ends being driven one in each of the adjacent timbers.

Iron Straps and Sockets are used to secure joints in wooden roofs and partitions, being forged or cast to the required shape.

Galvanising.—Iron nails and screws that are to be used in exposed positions are sometimes galvanised—that is, coated with a thin layer of zinc to prevent oxidation.

TOOLS

THE workshop should be furnished with the following tools, and the student should learn their names and be made acquainted with their use :—

SETTING-OUT TOOLS.

Two fold 2-feet Rule.
6-inch Try Square.
Bevel, with Steel Blade.
Straight-edge.
Plummet and Rule.
Spirit Level.

Chalk Line.
Pair of Compasses.
Mortice Gauge.
Marking Gauge.
Setting-out Knife.
Pair of Winding Strips.

CUTTING TOOLS.

Trying Plane, 22 inches long.
Jack Plane, 18 inches long.
Smoothing Plane.
Six Hollows.
Six Rounds.
$\frac{3}{4}$-inch Rebate Plane.
Plough and set of 8 irons, $\frac{1}{8}$ inch to $\frac{5}{8}$ inch.
Fillister.
Half Rip Saw, 3 teeth to inch.
Hand Saw, 4 ,, ,,
Tenon Saw, 8 ,, ,,
Dovetail Saw, 15 ,, ,,
Bow Saw.

Ten Firmer Chisels, $\frac{1}{8}$ inch to $1\frac{1}{2}$ inch.
Five Mortice Chisels, $\frac{1}{4}$ inch to $\frac{1}{2}$ inch.
Two Gouges, Small and Medium.
Slow-cutting Oil Stone.
Arkansas Stone Slip for Sharpening Hollows.
Oil Can and Salad Oil.
Cutting Gauge.
Spokeshave (Small).
Router.
Toothing Plane.
Scraper.

BORING TOOLS.

Brace and Set of Assorted Bits.
Three Gimlets.

Three Bradawls.

MISCELLANEOUS TOOLS.

Bench, with Iron chops.
24-inch Grindstone, mounted in Trough.
Glue Pot, Glue, and Glue Brush.
Joiner's Cramp, wrought-iron.
G Cramp.
Bench Holdfast.
Small and Large Hammers.

Two Screw-drivers, Small and Medium.
Two Punches.
Pair of Pincers.
Mallet.
Two Sawing Stools.
Two Hand Screws
Mitre-cuts.

Classification.—The tools employed for the working of timber may be broadly divided into four classes— viz. Setting-out, Cutting, Boring, and Miscellaneous :—

Setting-out Tools.—Those required for setting-out and testing the accuracy of work ; the chief among which are—the rule, the try and the set squares, the bevels, the compasses, the straight-edge, the plummet and rule, the spirit level, the chalk line, winding strips and gauges.

Rules.—The rule is employed for measuring up work or setting down dimensions. It consists usually of a thin strip of boxwood, 2 feet in length, divided into inches, eighths, and sixteenths, and in order to make it easily portable it is made to fold by means of hinged joints into a half, as shown in Fig. 13, or a fourth of its total length. If great lengths or large areas have to be measured rules 5 feet or 10 feet in length are employed, or metallic tapes, which are commonly made up to about 66 feet in length.

Squares.—The try square, as shown in Fig. 10, is used when shooting the edge of a board to test whether the same is square with a given surface, and also to set off lines on any surface at right angles to a given edge. It is composed of a steel blade (having two parallel edges) fixed at right angles to the edge of a wood stock, the latter having its square edge faced with brass to render it more durable. These are made with their blades from 2 inches to 1 foot in length ; beyond the latter dimension the whole of the square is usually made of some hard wood.

Set squares are employed to test if the angle between two surfaces (which are to be fixed either square or at any other angle with each other) is correct during the processes of fitting and fixing. They are also used in setting-out work requiring lines at right or oblique angles. If of sheet zinc, they are usually made up to about 9 inches length of edge ; when required larger they are of wood.

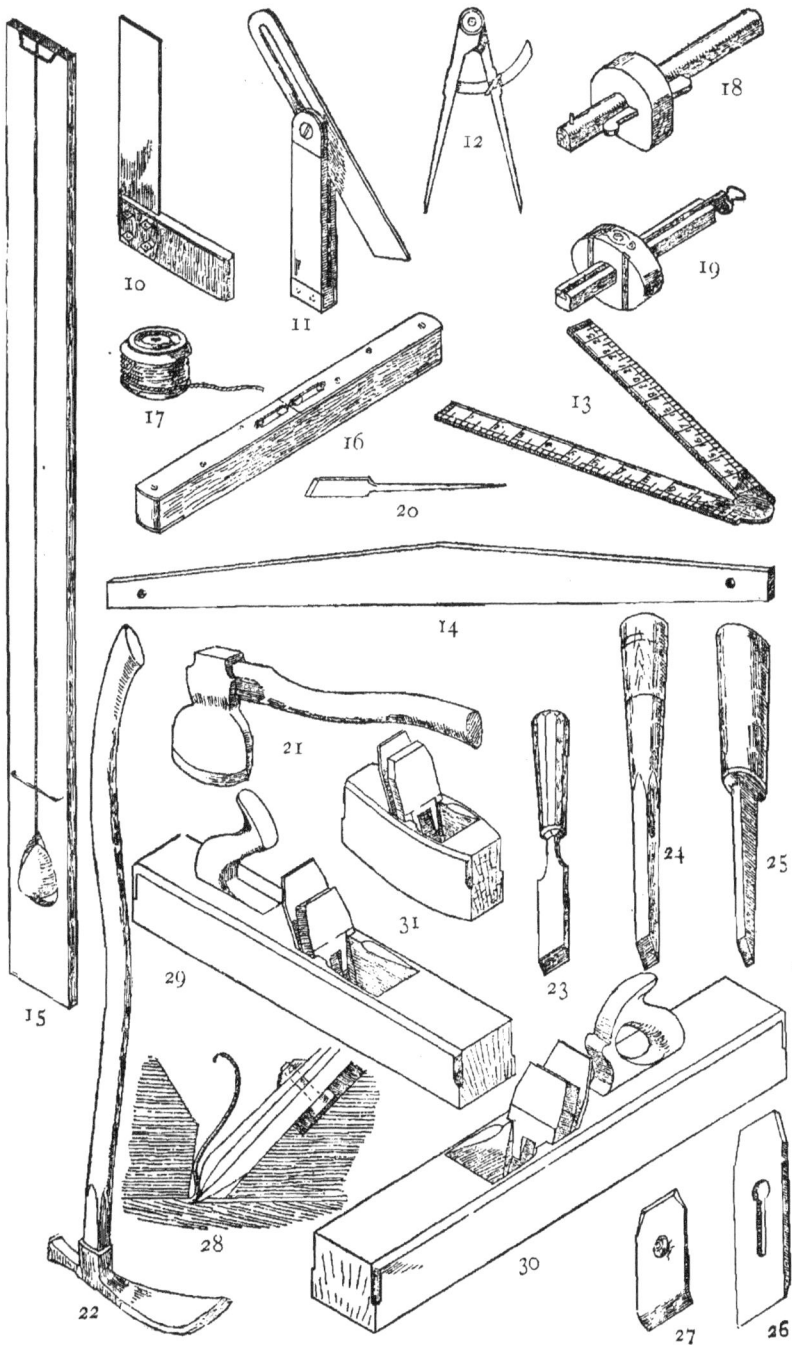

FIGS. 10 TO 31.—SETTING OUT TOOLS.

Bevels.—These are used for setting-out work and for testing the edges of boards required to be worked to any angle with the face. The bevel is formed of a steel blade with parallel edges, and having a slot extending from the centre to within a short distance of one extremity of the blade, and a wood stock, which has a cut down the centre equal to the thickness of the blade, the latter being placed in the cut in the stock and a screw passed through the stock and the slot in the blade, as shown in Fig. 11. The screw may be slackened or tightened, thus allowing the blade to be set at any angle. The slot in the blade enables the operator to fix the whole of the latter on one side of the stock. Bevels of large dimensions are made in wood.

Compasses.—These are employed for transferring distances and for scribing—*i.e.* drawing a line on any surface parallel to a given line on an irregular surface. There are two kinds, both entirely constructed of steel. In the first, as shown in Fig. 12, there is a thin member in the form of a quadrant attached to one leg and passing through a mortice in the second. The compasses when opened may be secured at any angle by a screw passing through the second leg and biting tightly against the side of the quadrant. In the second kind both legs are out of one piece of steel, the central portion being formed as a spring, which is so set that the natural tendency of the legs is to fly apart. The legs are kept together by a screw fixed to one leg and passing loosely through a hole drilled in the other, the distance being regulated by a fly-nut placed on the screw on the outside of the second leg. These, for general work, are inferior to the former kind, for, not being rigidly fixed, they are, while in use, likely to become altered.

Straight-edges.—Straight-edges, as illustrated in Fig. 14, are used for testing the accuracy of the work when forming plane surfaces, straight edges, and also for setting-out. They are prepared from American white pine, of all dimensions, those most convenient varying from 4 to 7 feet in length, 4 to 6 inches in width, and from ¾ inch to 1 inch in thickness. They require testing at frequent intervals to ensure accuracy.

The Plummet and Rule.—These, as shown in Fig. 15, are necessary when it is required to fix any piece of work vertically. The plummet consists of a piece of lead, oval in form, with a hole containing its longest axis, and by which a line is attached. The ordinary plummet weighs about 4 pounds, but for great depths heavier are to be preferred.

Where it is required to determine the position of one or a series of points perpendicularly above or below a given point, the plummet is often employed independently of the rule.

The plumb rule usually consists of a piece of straight grained white pine, about 5 feet long and 4 inches wide, the sides being perfectly parallel and straight ; a gauge line is marked along the middle of one face parallel with the sides ; a saw cut is made about ½ inch in length down the gauge line in the upper end of the rule in which the twine connected with the plummet is inserted ; a hole of a shape similar to that of the plummet, but much larger, is made in the rule about 6 inches from the bottom end, symmetrically about the gauge line. The plumb-line is inserted in the cut mentioned, and the plummet hangs freely in the hole. In fixing work, the plumb rule is placed against the face, and the whole adjusted until the plumb line exactly coincides with the gauge line on the rule ; this done, the work is secured. In fixing work in which the faces are battered, or in tapering, or entasised columns, the sides of the rule have to be shot to make the required angle with the centre line of the rule, or shaped to fit the face of the work to be fixed.

The Spirit Level.—This, as shown in Fig. 16, is

employed to adjust work requiring to be fixed perfectly horizontal. It consists of a wood stock ; the
under edge (which has to be applied to the work)
must be shot perfectly straight ; a mortice is sunk
in the upper edge for the reception of a glass bulb
containing spirits of wine. For ordinary purposes
this bulb consists of a tube about 4 inches in length
and about ⅜ inch in diameter. The tube is nearly
filled with spirit, leaving a small air bubble ; both
ends are then blown together in order to seal it her-
metically; the sides of the tube are not perfectly
straight, but slightly convex, thus facilitating the
movements of the air bulb. The glass is placed in
the mortice and set in plaster ; it is covered with a
slotted brass plate screwed to the wood, exposing
but a small portion of the glass. The brass plate
has a centre line marked, and the glass is so set that
when perfectly level the air bulb remains stationary,
and exactly central in the slot. The level may be
tested by turning it about on any plane surface until
the bulb is central ; a mark should then be made
on the surface, and the level turned about and applied
to the mark ; if the bulb still remains central the
level is correct. The stock should not be less than
9 inches in length ; in larger work it varies commonly
from 10 to 15 feet.

The Chalk Line.—This consists, as shown in
Fig. 17, of a length of fine twine, and is used to fix
a number of pieces of work in a straight line, or plane,
where the length of the whole arrangement is too
great to be spanned by a straight-edge, the latter
being generally preferred to a line. When in use
the line is strained between two known points, and
the other portions of the work adjusted to the line.
The line is also employed, when cutting up planks
of timber, for marking the cutting lines. In this
case, the line is chalked and strained between two
points previously determined ; the line is slightly

raised from the centre and then suddenly snapped, a chalk impression being left on the timber. This method is usually employed for marking the hard woods, the edges of the planks of which are generally irregular.

Winding Strips.—These are used in conjunction with the straight-edge in the preparation of timber for joinery as a test for accuracy when forming plane surfaces. They consist of two pieces of some hard wood (straight grained mahogany to be preferred); they run from 18 inches to 2 feet in length, about 2 inches in width, and about ½ inch thick; their edges are kept perfectly parallel. They are generally made feathered-edged—*i.e.* one edge thinner than the other, so that they taper in transverse section. The use of these will be described later.

Gauges.—These are employed for marking lines parallel to the edges or faces of pieces of stuff when thicknessing or taking them to a width. They consist of a stem and a movable fence; the stem is prepared from a piece of stuff about 9 inches in length and ¾ inch square, the top edges of the stem being rounded, and about ½ inch from one end a piece of steel wire is driven, the projecting point being filed to a sharp point. The fence consists of a piece of stuff about 2 inches square and ¾ inch thick; this has a hole through which the stem is passed; the fence may be secured at any point along the stem either by a wedge or screw. The drawing of a marking gauge is shown in Fig. 18. The mortice gauge, as shown in Fig. 19, is constructed similarly to the marking gauge, but has two teeth, one of which is movable, to allow it to be regulated at any required distance within its limits from the fixed tooth. It is used, in framing, for making two parallel marks preparatory to cutting the mortice and tenons.

The Striking Knife is a tool of the shape shown in Fig. 20. It is employed for making cut marks on stuff in setting-out work.

CUTTING TOOLS

Cutting tools for wood may be divided generally into two kinds—first, the paring or splitting tools for removing portions of the stuff in the direction of the fibres, such as axes, chisels, gouges, and planes ; and secondly, the saws, used to divide the wood in any direction.

The Axe.—There are two varieties of the axe in common use—the ordinary axe and the adze. The ordinary axe is employed by the carpenter for roughly removing extraneous portions of the work to be fixed or prepared. It consists of an iron head with a steel edge, of the shape shown in Fig. 21. The cutting edge of the axe is sharpened from both sides ; if the edge be in a bad condition it is first ground on a grindstone, the keen edge being finally produced by means of an oil-stone. When great precision is required a side-axe is employed. This is only sharpened on one side ; the flat side acts as a guide, and when slid along the surface of the stuff only takes off projecting portions ; more may be taken off by gently inclining the face of the axe towards the stuff. The adze (shown in Fig. 22) is a modified form of the side-axe ; it is used chiefly for roughly squaring logs of timber. The blade, or head, is slightly curved, and is sharpened on one side only ; the shaft is about 3 feet in length and is fixed at right angles to the face of the blade. In using the adze, the workman stands upon his work, grasps the adze with both hands, and plants his blows with great effect and precision upon the stuff beneath his feet.

Chisels.—The chisels are divided into three classes : Firmer chisels, socket chisels, and mortice chisels. Chisels for carpentry and joinery work are sharpened on one side only, in order to render them capable of cutting plane surfaces with approximate accuracy. The average length of the blades of chisels is about 6 inches. The firmer chisels have cast-steel blades, the socket and mortice have their blades of wrought-iron faced with steel. Wood working chisels have wood handles and are intended either to be propelled by the hand or driven by blows from a wood mallet —mallets are more effective than hammers in urging the chisels through the wood, and are less destructive to the handles. The firmer chisels, as shown in Fig. 23, have the thinnest blades, and though occasionally driven with mallets they are especially intended to receive their motive power from the pressure of the hand, and should be used for paring off small portions of the stuff only. The blades vary in width from $\frac{1}{16}$ to $1\frac{1}{2}$ inches ; the blades are often bevelled on their two long edges to enable the chisel to be worked into acute internal angles. The blade is fixed into the handle by means of a wedge-shaped tang, which is inserted into a hole bored into the handle ; the tang is prevented from splitting the handle by having a shoulder formed about its base, which keeps it from entering beyond its proper distance ; in addition to this the handle is often provided with a ferrule. The socket chisel, as shown in Fig. 24, differs from the firmer chisel in having a much thicker blade and in having a socket formed on its upper end, instead of a tang, for the reception of the handle. The socket chisel is used for rough carpenter's work and for large work generally. The mortice chisel, as shown in Fig. 25, as its name implies, is used for cutting mortices. It has a very stiff blade, the thickness usually being greater than the width, in order that it may withstand the violent cross stresses to which it is subjected. It is constructed similarly to the firmer chisel, the handle being fixed in the same manner.

Gouges.—Gouges are chisels the blades of which have been bent in their width to a curve. They are sharpened on one face only, and may be either inside or outside, which signifies that they are sharpened on the concave or convex face. Gouges are made as firmer or socket gouges, according as they are intended for light or for heavy work.

For wood carving, chisels and gouges are made to sharpen on both faces. The cutting edges are made of a great number of different shapes and sizes, and in many cases are bent in the direction of their length, in order to work in awkward corners and sunk or undercut surfaces.

Planes.—A plane is an apparatus in which the cutting iron is mounted, and its action modified so that the portion removed is of a uniform thickness. There is a great variety of planes constructed for various purposes, the principal among them being the jack plane, trying plane, smooth plane, rebate plane, shoulder plane, the bullnose, hollows and rounds, bead planes, compass plane, plough, fillister, and the spokeshave.

The jack, trying, and smooth planes are termed the bench planes, probably because they are used on nearly every piece of work that passes through the hands of the joiner. The object of these three planes is to reduce the rough sawn surfaces of timber to a smooth and even plane, this being accomplished by removing successive thin laminæ or shavings from the surface till the desired object is obtained. The arrangement of the cutting irons in the three planes is identical, being as follows:—First, the cutting irons, as shown in Fig. 26, vary from about 2 inches to $2\frac{1}{2}$ inches in width ; they are of wrought-iron, the lower end being faced with steel. They are ground on one side only. In forming the edge the mass of the metal is taken off with the grindstone, the keen edge being finally formed with the oil stone. In the roughest planes the irons are single, but the majority of planes have double irons. The second, or back iron, as shown in Fig. 27, is much shorter than the cutting iron, but is of the same width. It is sharpened in the same way, and as it has no actual cutting to perform it does not require sharpening after having been once set ; it also has a sharp curve in its length towards its lower edge. The hollow side of the back iron is placed against the face of the first iron, and is secured to it by means of a screw, the head of which passes through a hole and down a slot in the cutting iron ; the slot in the first iron allows the second to be adjusted as the first is worn away. The iron is fixed in the plane in an inclined position by means of a wedge, the inclination varying between 45° and 60°, those with the steeper pitch being used for hard woods ; the latter have, to a certain extent, a scraping action combined with the cutting.

The thickness of the shaving in planes having single irons is regulated by the width of the mouth of the plane, but owing to the cut caused by the iron having a tendency to extend in advance of the cutting edge a splitting or tearing action is induced. The cleft runs in the direction of the grain, and if not parallel to the surface planed, the shaving is liable to become thicker and so choke the mouth of the plane, causing a ragged and torn surface. To obviate this defect the back iron is employed. This is screwed to the cutting iron and has its edge close to the cutting edge, as shown in Fig. 28, the distance between the two edges varying with the fineness or coarseness of the shaving required. The back iron has the effect of breaking the shaving immediately after it commences to rise up the cutting edge by suddenly changing its direction, as shown in Fig. 28, and thus the shaving, having no stiffness nor length, has no leverage, and consequently no power to raise the grain in front of the cutting edge. In order to obtain a plane surface it is necessary that the cutting edge should be accurately sharpened. The edge should not be exactly straight, but form a segment of a very large circle, in order that the corners may not enter the surface at every stroke ; the edge should on no account be concave.

The cutting edge of any bench plane iron is sharpened by pushing it rapidly backwards and forwards in an inclined position on an oil stone, the angle of inclination being maintained constant throughout the operation, the upper part of the plane iron being held firmly in the right hand, and the lower in the left, the iron being guided with the right hand, and the pressure applied with the left. When the iron is rubbed down sufficiently, it is wiped and stropped on the palm of the left hand to remove the loose steel remaining on the edge after sharpening. To remove the iron from the plane, a smart tap with the hammer on the top of the front end of the plane in the case of the jack and the trying, or on the back end in the case of the smoothing plane, is sufficient to loosen the wedge. To set the iron, it is placed in position and held there with the thumb of the left hand ; the operator glances down the face, and regulates the iron with his right hand until the edge is just visible above the surface. The wedge is then inserted and tightened by a few gentle taps with the hammer. This done, the iron can be set coarser or finer by gently tapping either the top of the iron or the end of the plane.

In order that the bench planes shall work correctly, it is necessary that the plane of the wearing faces be accurately kept ; in order to do this they will require shooting at intervals, to correct any inaccuracy arising from warping of the stuff or from wear. While a plane is being shot, it should have its iron wedged into position with its cutting edge

slightly below the surface, as a difference is likely
to arise through the stock springing or bending
slightly when the wedge is driven in. After much
wear and successive shootings, the mouth of the
plane grows wider ; as the opening is one factor in
determining the thickness of the shaving, it becomes
necessary to repair the face, which is done by letting
in small pieces of some hard wood, such as box or
ebony, to reduce the size of the opening. It is common
in smoothing planes to have the front half of the
plane of iron fixed in such a manner that the mouth
can be regulated, but these are not to be recommended,
owing to the unequal rate of wear of the iron and
wood in the face ; it is always far better to have
the whole of the face of iron.

Jack Plane.—The jack plane consists of a wood
stock, as shown in Fig. 29 ; it is about 17 inches
in length and about 3 inches square in cross-section,
having a rectangular hole for the reception of the
iron of the shape shown in the figure, and to allow
for the egress of the shaving. At the back of the
stock there is a handle projecting from the upper
surface. This handle is grasped and the plane is
propelled by the right hand ; any extra pressure
required is imparted by the left hand, which also
guides the tool in the forward stroke. The especial
use of the jack plane is to remove the rough sawn
surface of stuff, and to bring it to an approximately
plane surface preparatory to trying it up.

The Trying Plane.—The trying plane, as shown in
Fig. 30, differs from the jack plane in having a longer
stock, and also a modification of the handle to increase
its strength. The usual length of the stock is 1 foot
10 inches but they are made much longer when
extreme accuracy is required, as where the edges
of boards are jointed ; they are then termed jointing
planes. The section of the stock is about $3\frac{1}{4}$ inches
square, and the iron $2\frac{1}{2}$ inches in width. The trying

plane is held and used in a similar manner to the
jack plane. Its particular use is to form plane, true
surfaces and to shoot edges of boards straight. Owing
to its great length, it is unable to enter the hollows
of any irregular surface; and can only take off the
projecting portions. The plane is worked over the
surface until a continuous shaving can be taken off
in any direction. The process of planing up a surface will be fully explained later.

Smoothing Plane.—The smoothing plane has a
stock of the shape shown in Fig. 31 ; it is 8 inches
in length, and about 3 inches in width at the widest
part ; the width of the iron is about 2¼ inches. The
smoothing plane is used to put a finish on the work
when it is together, by taking off a fine shaving from
the already true surfaces.

The Rebate Plane.—This plane consists of a rectangular stock, as shown in Fig. 32, about 9 inches
in length, about 3½ inches in width, and varying from
about ½ inch to 1½ inches in thickness. It differs from
the planes already described chiefly in the provision
made for ejecting the shaving, and in having the iron
the whole width of the face. The mouth of the plane
and the cutting edge of the iron are on the skew,
in order that a cleaner cut may be made. There is
a conical shaped hole in the side of the plane, a short
distance above the face, from which the shaving is
thrown out, this action being automatic owing to
the shape of the hole. The rebate plane, as its name
implies, is employed for forming rebates in the edges
of boards or pieces of stuff.

The Shoulder Plane.—This is usually of metal, either
gun-metal or steel, and is of the shape shown in
Fig. 33, being from 6 inches to 7 inches in length.
It is similar in principle to the rebate plane, the
cutting edge of the iron extending over the whole
width of the face ; but it is square, not on the skew
as in the previous example. The iron has a pitch

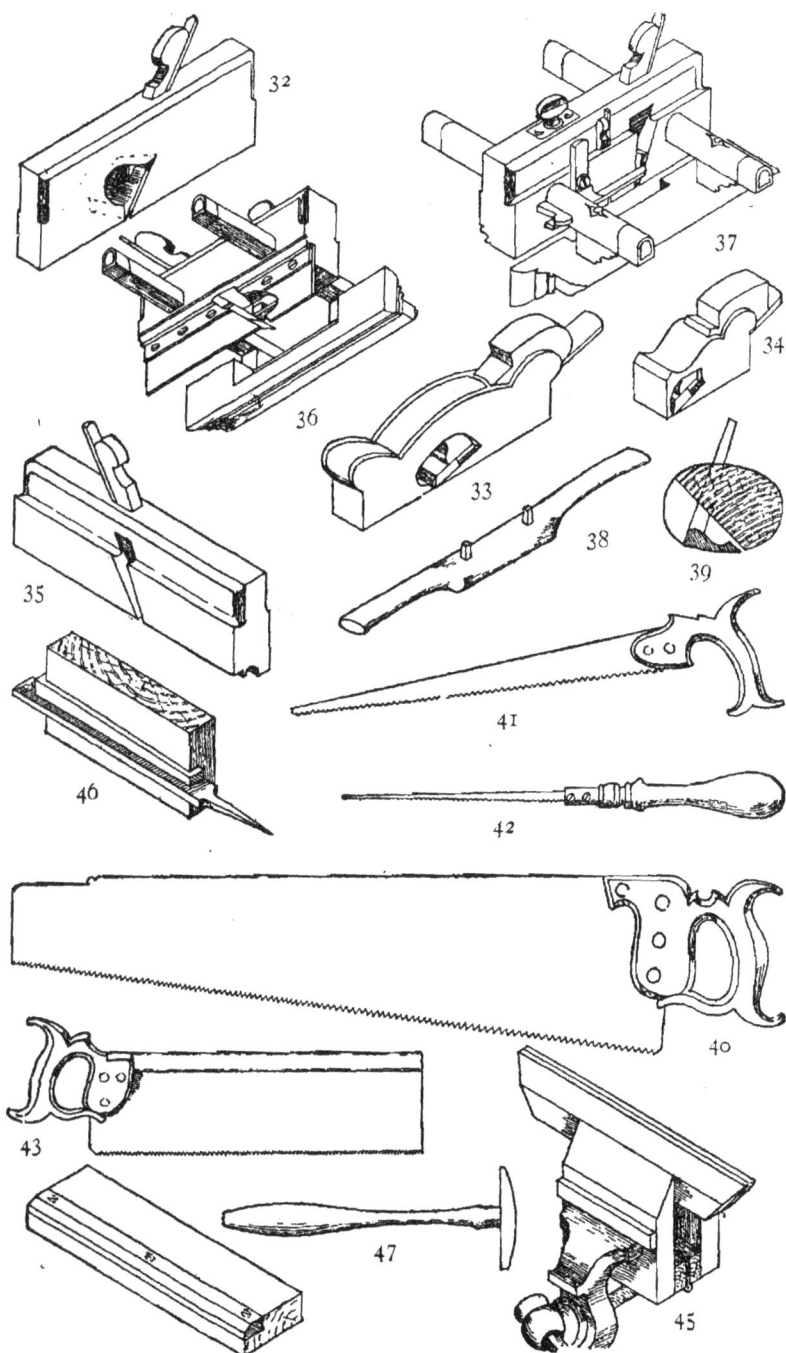

FIGS. 32 TO 43, AND 45 TO 47.—CUTTING TOOLS.

D

of about 25°, and is fixed in the plane with the face containing the cutting edge downwards. The mouth is extremely fine, and allows only a very thin shaving to pass through. The plane is specially designed to cut across the grain.

The Bullnose.—This plane is similar to the shoulder plane, but shorter, the chief difference being that the cutting edge is taken to within about $\frac{3}{16}$ inch of the front end of the plane. Its special object is to finish a flat surface which ends abruptly against some projecting member. The bullnose is shown in Fig. 34.

Another plane designed for a similar purpose to the bullnose, termed the chariot plane, is employed. The chariot differs from the bullnose in that the cutting iron does not extend over the whole width of the face.

Hollows and Rounds.—These planes are designed to work mouldings. The planes are made in pairs, having their faces worked to a segment of a circle. They are made in eighteen different sizes. The stock is about 9 inches in length, about $3\frac{1}{2}$ inches in width, and varies in thickness from about $\frac{1}{4}$ inch to 2 inches, according to the number. The irons may be fixed square or on the skew. The shaving escapes through an opening made in one side. These planes are similar to that shown in Fig. 35.

Bead and Moulding Planes.—These planes are identical in principle and construction with the hollows and rounds, differing only in having the reverse of a moulding worked on their faces instead of a plain segment. Fig. 35 is an illustration of a bead plane.

Compass Plane.—This plane is constructed similarly to an ordinary smoothing plane, but having its face worked in the direction of its length into a segment of a circle. It is used to work internal circular surfaces. Compass planes are now usually made in iron ; the face consists of a thin sheet of flexible steel. Its advantage is that it may be adjusted within certain limits to a large number of curves, both convex and concave.

Plough.—An illustration of the plough is shown in Fig. 36. Its object is to form grooves in wood parallel to the face edge. It consists of a stock about 9 inches in length and about 3 inches in width. To the lower part of this is attached a thin steel plate to steady the cutting iron and regulate the thickness of the shaving. At the side of this plate is a movable stop to regulate the depth of the groove. It may be adjusted by means of a thumb-screw on the top of the stock to which it is connected, to any distance from the cutting edge up to its limit, and it may be fixed in its position by a set screw on the side of the stock. A movable fence is attached to the stock by two arms, the object being to regulate the distance of the groove from the edge of the stuff. The stock is fixed at any point along the arms by means of wedges as shown. A set of eight irons is usually supplied with every plough, which vary in width by $\frac{1}{16}$ from $\frac{1}{8}$ inch to $\frac{5}{8}$ inch.

Fillister.—This tool is practically a rebate plane to which is attached a movable fence, as shown in Fig. 37. The arrangement for the egress of the shaving is modified. A movable stop to regulate the depth of the rebate similar to the one on the plough is also affixed. In the better kinds, a vertical knife is fixed on the inside edge in advance of the cutting iron ; this prevents a ragged cut in stuff that is not straight grained, and ensures a clean, sharp edge to the rebate. This tool is employed for working rebates on the back edges of narrow pieces of stuff such as sash styles.

Spokeshave.—This tool is designed to work sharp curves, either internal or external. It consists, as shown in Fig. 38, of a wood stock, to the central portion of which a knife about 3 inches in length is attached. The wood stock terminates at both ends in a handle. The knife is turned up at both ends and passes through holes in the stock made to receive them. Fig. 39 shows a section through the centre of the stock and the knife.

Saws.—A saw consists of a thin steel blade having a serrated edge formed by a number of triangular teeth worked on the blade, the front edges of which act as so many knives. During every stroke of the saw each tooth individually cuts or tears a path for itself, and thus leaves a fresh surface for its successor to work upon, and by a repetition of such strokes a piece of timber may be severed in any direction.

The saws of the joiner may be classified as follows :—(1) tapering saws, (2) back saws, (3) frame saws. Under the first heading there is the half rip saw, the hand saw, the panel saw, the table saw, and the pad saw. Under the second there is the tenon and the dovetail saw. Under the third there is the frame or bow saw. The teeth are triangular in shape, the cutting edge usually being kept at right angles to the back of the saw.

Half Rip Saw.—The half rip saw is of the shape shown in Fig. 40. It consists of a thin steel blade slightly thinner on the back edge than on the front, to allow it to clear itself easily in the cut. The blade is about 28 inches in length, and about 9 inches at its wide and 4 inches at its narrow end. It has about three and a half teeth to the inch. The special use of the half rip saw is to cut wood in the direction of the grain, for which purpose it has large teeth, as the resistance of the stuff in this direction is slight compared to that in a cut in the transverse direction.

Hand Saw.—This saw is constructed similarly to the rip saw. The blade is 26 inches in length, and about $7\frac{1}{2}$ inches at the wide end, and 3 inches at the narrow end ; it has from five to six teeth to the inch. The use of the hand saw is to cut stuff across the fibres, but it is also used for general purposes.

The Panel Saw.—This is of a shape similar to that of the hand saw. The blade is 24 inches in length, 7 inches at the wide end, 2½ inches at the narrow end, and has about seven teeth to the inch. It is used for cross-cutting thin stuff, or where the jarring of a coarser saw would tend to split the stuff or would be detrimental to the work.

The Table Saw.—This saw is of the shape shown in Fig. 41. It has a tapering blade about 15 inches in length; it is about 2 inches at the wide end, and about ¾ inch at the narrow end. The number of teeth varies from about seven to five to the inch. The use of the table saw is to work about curves of a fairly large radius.

The Pad Saw.—This saw is shown in Fig. 42. It has a blade about 1 foot in length, and from ½ inch in width at the wide end to ⅛ inch at the narrow end, and has about nine teeth to the inch. The use of this saw is to work about very small curves. Owing to the delicacy of the blade, and consequently its liability to breakage, provision is made to slide it back into the handle when not in use to protect it. The blade is fixed in position when ready for use by the set screws shown.

The Tenon Saw.—The tenon saw has a much thinner blade than those previously described, and in order to stiffen it a heavy piece of brass or iron is folded over the back, as shown in Fig. 43. In these saws the depth of the cut cannot exceed the width of the blade ; they are therefore made parallel so as to obtain the maximum depth of cut. The ordinary length of the blade is 14 inches, and from 3 inches to 4 inches in width. It has about twelve teeth to the inch. Its special use is to make fine cuts across the grain, such as in cutting the shoulders of tenons

Dovetail Saw.—The dovetail saw is practically similar in principle to the tenon saw, the only differences

being its smaller dimensions and a slight modification of the handle ; the blade is from 6 inches to
8 inches in length ; it is very thin, and has about
sixteen teeth to the inch. Its use, as its name implies,
is to cut dovetails, and to make very fine cuts.

Bow Saws.—These saws are of the shape shown
in Fig. 44 ; their object is to make curved cuts.
In order to pass about very sharp curves the blades
must be very fine and narrow ; they vary from about
$\frac{1}{8}$ inch to $\frac{3}{8}$ inch in width, and have from about twelve
to eighteen teeth to the inch. As the blades possess
very little stiffness, they are fixed in a frame as shown,
and are subjected to a tensional stress by twisting
the string fixed to the opposite ends of the sides
to which the saw is fixed.

Saw Sharpening.—Every saw, after being used for
a short time, requires the cutting edges of its teeth
renewed. As it is impracticable to apply a stone
to the cutting edges of the teeth of a saw for the
purpose of renewing them, after they have become
dulled, a three square file is employed, the size of
the latter varying with the size of the teeth to be
filed. The teeth may be simply filed and the edges
renewed, or, if in a bad condition, they may require
remodelling. The latter operation is necessary at
certain intervals for the following reason—the two
extremities of a saw rarely get used, the central
portion only getting much worn ; in filing the teeth
more is taken from the centre than from the ends,
to bring the teeth at that part to a state of efficiency ;
the edge of the saw thus tends to become concave
or irregular. Thus the sharpening process may be
classified under two heads : first, when the teeth
require remodelling ; and secondly, when they require
to be retouched between the intervals of the former.

There are two general operations in sharpening a
saw—viz. (1) filing, and (2) setting the teeth ; the
first is to renew the cutting edges, and the second

consists in bending the teeth alternately to the right and left of the cutting edge ; the object of the latter being to make the cut sufficiently large to prevent the blade of the saw from binding in the cut.

In filing the teeth, the following points should be kept in view :—First, every tooth should be of a similar form ; secondly, every tooth should be of a similar size, or, as in the case of tapering saws where the teeth slightly diminish towards the point, the reduction in size should be gradual and uniform ; thirdly, the cutting edge of a saw should be perfectly straight ; on no account should it be concave, but it may without disadvantage be slightly convex if the curve be kept perfectly uniform and does not change suddenly at any point in the length ; the object of forming an edge convex is to correct the tendency of the latter becoming concave after retouching.

In setting the teeth the following points should be considered :—First, every tooth should be inclined or bent over towards the opposite side to the one preceding it ; secondly, every tooth should receive a uniform amount of set ; thirdly, the smaller the amount of set compatible with efficiency the better.

Supposing a saw to be in a bad condition, the following four operations in their respective order would be gone through to effectively renew the cutting edge : (1) levelling, (2) remodelling, (3) setting, (4) sharpening.

Levelling.—The saw is gripped in a pair of saw-clamps, a common form of which is shown in Fig. 45 ; these have wood jaws from about 9 inches to 12 inches in length ; the edge is then rubbed down—*i.e.* levelled with a flat file which is fixed with its cutting face at right angles to a piece of stuff which serves as a guide, as shown in Fig. 46. With this the whole cutting edge may be made perfectly straight or slightly convex as desired.

After the edge has been straightened it will be found that the apices of nearly all the teeth have been rubbed away, and some very much more than others, thus rendering necessary the remodelling of the same, which is the next operation.

Remodelling.—The process of remodelling the teeth is conducted as follows :—The saw is fixed in the clamps commencing at one end of the blade and having the teeth projecting above the clamp sufficient to prevent the latter interfering with the use of the file. The file is then taken, the point between the thumb and fingers of the left hand and the handle in the right. The file is held perfectly horizontal, with its faces inclined at the right angle, and in using it should be pushed through firmly from point to haft at each forward stroke and perpendicularly to the face of the saw, and should be raised clear of the work at every return ; about six teeth are taken to commence with, a different tooth being operated upon at every stroke ; these are filed till they have been reduced to their triangular form again and the facets formed by the rubbing down have disappeared, care being taken to finish number one tooth first, and then as each tooth is completed a fresh one is commenced, and this operation is repeated until all the teeth have been treated. At intervals in the process, the file should be placed in the first tooth to ensure the faces of the file retaining their original inclinations in the operator's grasp ; by these means every tooth may be formed to the correct shape.

Setting.—A setting-block and hammer, as shown in Fig. 47, are required for this process. The setting-block is of wood, having on one edge of its upper face a strip of bar-iron let in flush and screwed to the block ; a chamfer is taken off the edge of the iron, making about 20° with the face of the block. The blade of the saw is placed flat on the top face of the block, with the teeth projecting over the chamfer a distance depending on the amount of set required, and every alternate tooth is then given a smart blow with one point of the hammer. When every alternate tooth on one side is bent the saw is turned over and the process repeated. Many setting-blocks have movable guides to regulate the distance the teeth shall overhang the chamfer. There are several other contrivances for setting saws, the chief among which consists of a plate of steel with a number of cuts varying in thickness in the edge to accommodate them to blades of varying thicknesses. The setting is accomplished by inserting the teeth one by one into one of the cuts mentioned, and then depressing one end of the set and so bending the tooth. It is difficult to obtain uniformity by this method, and the teeth are very apt to break unless the greatest care is exercised by glancing at the cutting edge from the back of the blade. It may be easily seen if the setting is uniform. The setting of a saw is a very important operation, and the correctness with which it is done materially affects the efficiency of the saw. If the setting is generally irregular, it causes the saw to jump and make a ragged cut ; if there is more on one side than on the other, the saw has a tendency to run in the direction of the side that has the most set ; and, if there is too much set, a coarse ragged cut is made, the cutting goes on slowly, and the teeth become dulled rapidly.

Sharpening.—After the setting the sharpening proper commences. The saw is fixed in the clamps as in the remodelling process, beginning at the back end of the blade ; the file is held in the hands as before, but inclined point upwards at an angle of about 10° to the horizontal, and at the same time it is inclined at about 80° to the blade in plan with the point towards the handle of the saw. In this position the file should be pushed firmly forward from point to handle in every alternate incision between the teeth ; one or two strokes may be sufficient to sharpen each tooth, but as nearly as possible the same number should be given to each tooth to prevent a lack of uniformity. Care should be taken to send each stroke straight from end to end, and not to let the file rock or change its direction in its forward motion ; it is also important that the file should be steadily pressed downwards, so as to remove an equal amount of material from each side of the incision that is being operated upon ; if the file be pressed more against one side of the incision than against the other, the teeth will rapidly become irregular. The file should be lifted clear of the saw at every return stroke to prevent destroying the burr formed on the teeth and to economise the file. Every incision on both sides of the saw is treated as described, and when this is accomplished the saw is ready for use.

If the saw only requires touching up, the last process is all that is necessary.

BORING TOOLS

THE following are the chief among the boring tools :
the bradawl, the gimlet, the auger, the brace and
bits ; among the latter there are the centre bit, the
twist bit, the nose bit, the spoon bit, the quill bit,
the rose countersink, the metal countersink, and the
ordinary countersink.

Bradawl.—The bradawl is of the form shown in
Fig. 48. It is used for boring holes in soft wood ;
it may be worked by the pressure of the hand only,
or it may be driven by a hammer or mallet, in which
case the edge of the bradawl should be placed across
the fibres, and not in the same direction ; if this be
not done, the tendency will be to split the fibres.
The bradawl is only useful for small holes.

Gimlet.—For boring small holes in hard wood the
gimlet is employed. There are two kinds of gimlets,
as shown in Figs. 49 and 50, the plain and the twist
gimlet. The plain hollow or shell gimlet is the better
for hard woods, as its action is slower than that of
the twist gimlet ; the advantage of the twist gimlet
is that it removes the stuff as it is cut, but it has a
greater tendency to split the material.

Auger.—Augers are large gimlets with a long stem
and a movable handle about 1 foot in length, intended to be used with both hands. There are two
kinds of augers—the shell and the screw. The shell
augers are similar to the gimlets (Fig. 49), and
require considerable pressure to urge them forward
in addition to that expended in turning them. The
screw augers, as shown in Fig. 51, are provided with
a screw point which enters by itself ; they are provided with cutting edges, and the helical surfaces
remove the waste product.

Brace.—The brace is a tool of the form shown in Fig. 52, its object being to facilitate and increase the speed of the revolutions of boring tools. They are formed of wood or steel, the latter material being preferred owing to its greater strength. Braces vary slightly in the arrangement for securing the bits. Many of the braces, especially those of wood, have simply a square socket and a spring catch ; in these the bits must be fitted to the socket. The steel braces usually have an expansible square socket, which can be adjusted to any bit.

Centre Bit.—The centre bit is of the shape shown in Fig. 53 ; it consists of a triangular pin in the centre, a vertical knife edge and a horizontal cutter ; the knife edge slightly projects beyond the latter, and when the bit is made to revolve it makes a clean, circular cut, the stuff from the interior of which is removed by the cutter in the form of a helical shaving. The centre bit is not well adapted for boring with the grain.

Twist Bits.—Twist bits are exactly similar to the screw auger, but are shorter, and have their ends adapted for fitting in the brace.

The Nose Bit.—This bit, as shown in Fig. 54, is formed of a circular piece of steel, hollowed out at the lower end, and provided at its extremity with a transverse cutter. It is specially adapted for boring with the grain.

The Spoon Bit.—The spoon bit is formed similarly to the nose bit, but does not possess the transverse cutter, and is rounded at the point, as shown in Fig. 55. It is used for boring with the grain.

The Quill Bit.—The quill bit is formed similarly to the nose bit. It does not possess the transverse cutter, the end being finished as shown in Fig. 56. The extremities and edges of the hollowed out portion are sharp, in order to cut the fibres, the object of this bit being to bore holes across the fibres.

Countersinks.—These are employed for forming a conical sinking in the end of a hole to receive a screw head.   There are three kinds: (1) the rose, (2) the

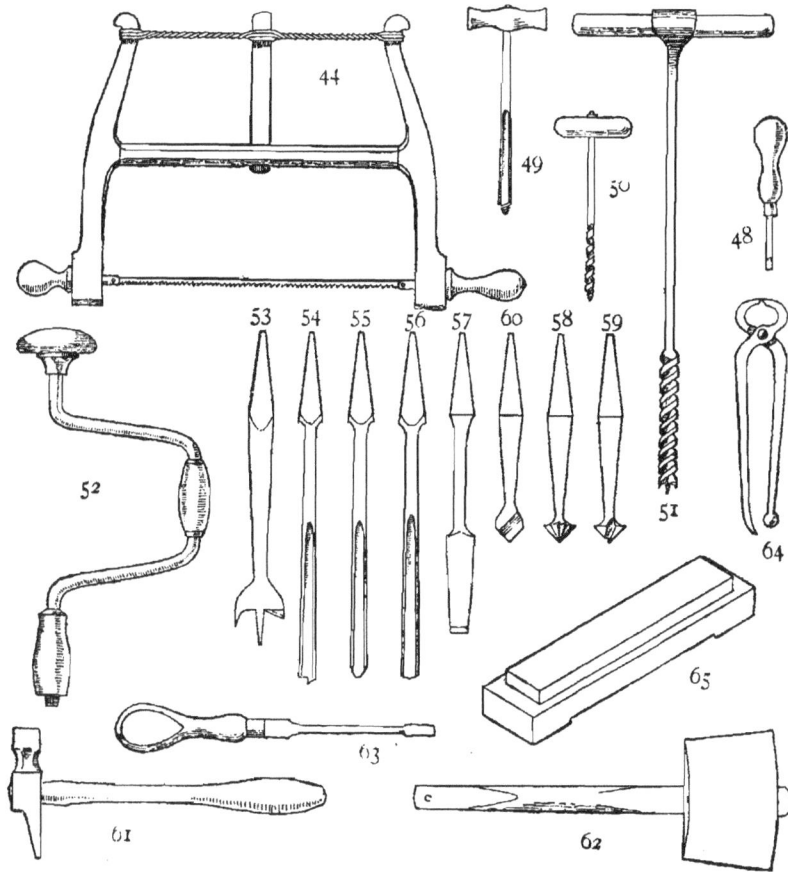

FIGS. 44, 48 TO 65.

metal, and (3) the ordinary or soft wood countersink.

1. *The Rose.*—This bit is shown in Fig. 58.   The conical end has a serrated surface forming a number of cutters.   This bit is used for countersinking holes in hard woods, or in soft metals such as brass.

2. *The Metal.*—This bit is formed similarly to an

ordinary metal drill, as shown in Fig. 60 ; it is used for countersinking holes in iron.

3. *The Soft Wood.*—This tool has a plain conical end with one sinking, as shown in Fig. 59 ; its action is very rapid, and it is consequently only adapted for soft woods.

Screw-driver Bit.—This is shown in Fig. 57.

MISCELLANEOUS TOOLS

In addition to the tools previously mentioned, there are a number which cannot be classified under any special category, but have uses peculiar to themselves. Among these are the hammer, the mallet, the screw-driver, the punch, the pincers, and the oil stone and slips.

Hammer.—Fig. 61 shows the type of hammer usually employed by the joiner, who is ordinarily provided with three sizes for light, medium, or for heavy work.

Mallet.—The mallet is a wooden hammer, used for driving chisels with wood handles ; those used by the joiner are of the shape shown in Fig. 62 ; the workman usually has two mallets—one for light bench work and another for heavy work, such as morticing.

The Screw-driver.—The screw-driver, as its name implies, is used for turning screws. Fig. 63 shows the type usually employed.

The Punch.—The punch consists of a short piece of steel bar, square or octagonal in section, forged and hardened similarly to a chisel, but having a small rectangular facet instead of a point. It is employed for imparting the finishing blows to nails, to prevent the surface of the wood becoming bruised by the face of the hammer, or in driving the nail head below the surface.

The Pincers.—The pincers are shown in Fig. 64 ; they are employed for extracting nails which have bent or are taking a wrong direction whilst being driven.

The Oil Stone.—Oil stones are pieces of soft, finely grained sandstone, employed to work the keen edge on cutting tools ; they are cut to convenient sized pieces, about 9 by 1¾ by 1¼ inches, which are usually encased in wood, as shown in Fig. 65, to prevent breakage and for cleanliness. The following stones, named from the places whence they are obtained, are in most general use : (1) the Canada stone, (2) the Washita stone, (3) the Charnley Forest stone, (4) the Arkansas stone, (5) the Turkey stone.

1. *Canada.*—This stone is rather coarse, of a greyish colour, soft, and quick cutting ; is rapidly worn away ; it is not good for tools requiring a very keen edge.

2. *The Washita.*—This stone is close grained, whitish in colour, fairly soft, and quick cutting ; will work a finer edge than the Canada, and is largely used among carpenters.

3. *Charnley Forest.*—This is a close-grained stone of a greyish tint tinged with red ; it is fairly hard and not very quick cutting ; it will work a very fine edge sufficiently keen for joiner's work.

4. *The Arkansas.*—This has a very fine grain, is of a whitish colour ; it is hard, wears away slowly, and is slow cutting ; it is used where an extremely keen edge is required.

5. *Turkey Stone* is very fine grained, varies in colour from white to black ; it is soft, wears quickly, cuts rapidly, and will work a keen edge.

Slips.—These are small pieces of oil stone, with shaped edges ; they are used for sharpening shaped cutting edges, such as for gouges and the irons for moulding planes ; they are prepared from any of the above-mentioned stones.

Bench.—The full size joiner's bench is 12 feet in length, 2 feet 9 inches wide, and 2 feet 9 inches high. The top consists of two 11-inch by 2-inch boards, and one 11-inch by 1 inch centre-board. To stiffen the edges vertical boards 1½ by 9 inches are placed the full length of each long edge ; these are attached to two strong frames, each consisting of

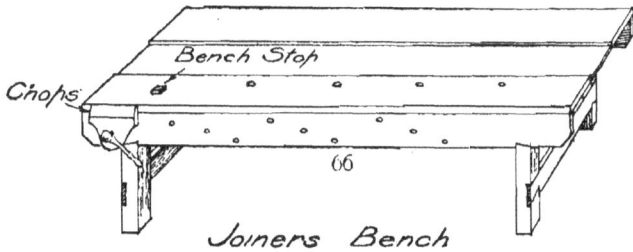

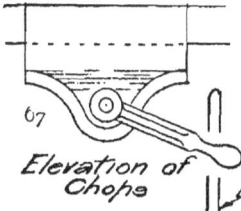

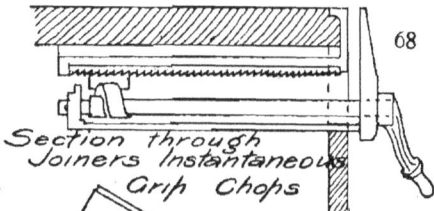

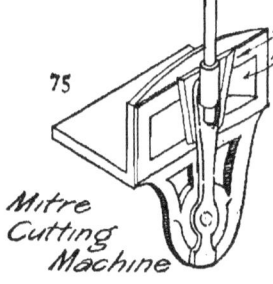

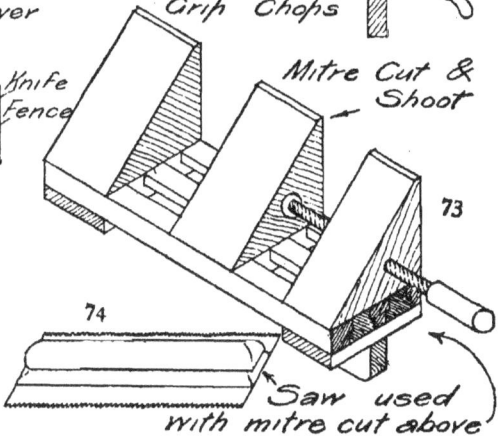

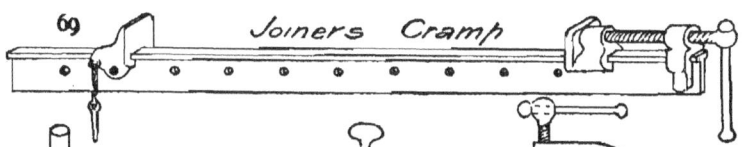

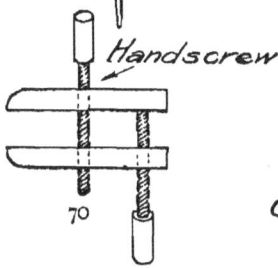

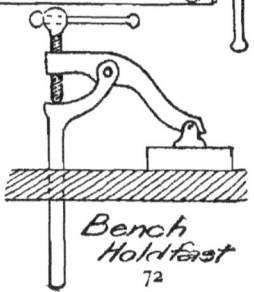

Bench Stop

Chops

66

Joiners Bench

67

Elevation of
Chops

68

Section through
Joiners Instantaneous
Grip Chops

Lever

Knife

Fence

75

Mitre Cut &
Shoot

Mitre
Cutting
Machine

73

74

Saw used
with mitre cut above

69   Joiners Cramp

Handscrew

70

G. Cramp
71

Bench
Holdfast
72

FIGS. 66 TO 75.

E

two legs and two rails, each frame being fixed one foot from the ends of the bench. The bench is provided with a vice or chops near to one end, to hold stuff rigidly while being worked. These may be of wood, adjusted by a screw, or better, of iron, of the form shown in Figs. 66, 67, and 68, known as the instantaneous grip vice, which is designed with a cam and rack to increase the rapidity with which work may be secured. A series of holes are drilled in the side board, in which pegs are inserted to support the edges of boards secured in the vice. A stop, consisting of a piece of oak 12 inches by 2 inches by 2 inches, is fitted tightly in a 2-inch by 2-inch perforation near to one end of the top, as shown. The amount of projection can be adjusted with a hammer, the object being to prevent work sliding while being planed. A series of holes are bored in the top to accommodate a bench holdfast.

Cramps.—Fig. 69 shows a joiner's iron cramp, employed for drawing the parts together while glueing up framing. Figs. 70 and 71 show a hand-screw and a G cramp used for temporarily holding parts together.

Bench Holdfast.—Fig. 72 shows a bench holdfast, employed for temporarily securing stuff to a bench while being worked.

Mitre-Cut and Shoot.—Fig. 73 shows a mitre-cut and shoot, employed for forming mitres in wide or moulded pieces of stuff; and Fig. 74 illustrates the special saw, consisting of a blade with teeth cut on both edges and having a handle screwed on one face.

Mitre-Cutting Machine.—Fig. 75 shows an iron mitre-cutting machine ; this is screwed to the edge of a bench. The stuff to be mitred is placed against the fence with the end protruding beyond the path of the knife, which latter is actuated by the hand pressing the lever.

OPERATIONS

Sawing.—By sawing is understood the separation
or cutting of material by means of a saw.

In using the saw, note the following points :—

(1) The stuff should be kept in a rigid position,
as, for instance, upon two stools, with the weight

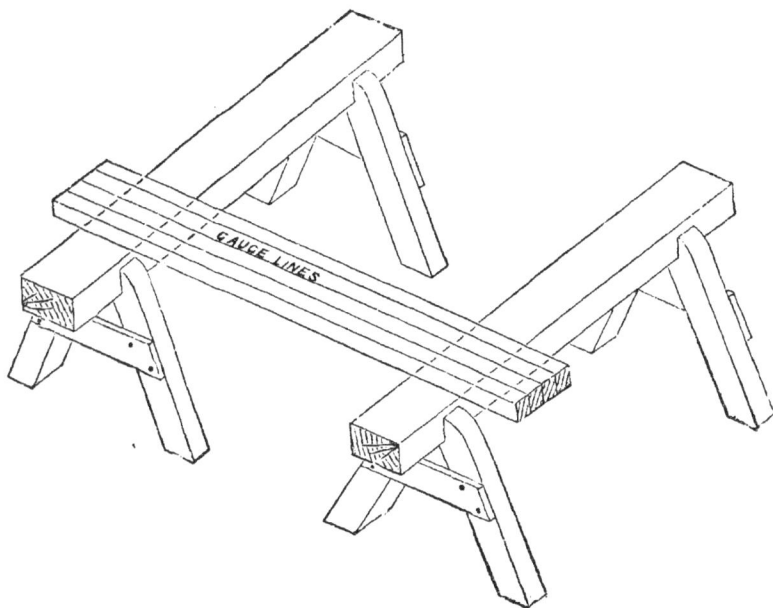

FIG. 76.

of the operator pressing upon it, or it may be fixed
in the bench vice.

(2) The cut is made by the forward stroke, which
should be given with a uniform pressure. Care must
be exercised (except in the case of the bow and pad
saws) that the movements of the saw are such that
the surface of the saw, from the beginning to the
finish of the cut, is in one plane, any departure from
this condition causing the saw to buckle.

Take a piece of stuff—say, a deal 12 feet long, 9 inches wide, 2 inches thick of northern pine, place it on two stools, as shown in Fig. 76, with the clean, wide face uppermost. Make parallel black-lead lines to and from the straighter face edge, dividing the face into four equal parts. This may be readily accomplished by notching slips of wood to the required distances, as $2\frac{1}{4}$, $4\frac{1}{2}$, or $6\frac{3}{4}$ inches. Take a half rip saw, and begin cutting, being careful to keep the face of the saw vertical. If properly sawn, the edges will be square with the faces.

If the edges of the plank are irregular, the cutting lines must be marked with chalk by a chalk line, or with a black-lead pencil and a straight-edge.

Planing.—This is the name given to the operation of preparing a smooth plane surface by means of planes ; all irregularities, projections, or woolliness left by the saw on the face of the work being removed.

Take a piece of stuff—say, American pine, about 2 feet long, $4\frac{1}{2}$ inches wide, and 2 inches thick. Remove the rough from one wide face with the jack plane, and reduce to a perfect plane surface with a trying plane, testing with the winding strips as follows :

Place the winding strips at each end, look to see if one corner is higher than the other ; the winding strips being wider than the board will multiply the error, if any, and this is readily seen when one eye is closed and the other is comparing the two upper edges of winding strips. If one corner—say A—appears high, the thickness at that and at the opposite corner B should be measured, and that part of the face nearer the thicker of the two should be planed down to equal the thickness of the opposite corner. Apply winding strips, as shown in Fig. 77, and if the same corner should still appear high take off equally on the face at A and B till the winding strips appear level. Plane the surface, so that a straight-edge applied between any two points is resting wholly on the surface, and the trued surfaces at corners A and B are retained.

Place the stuff in the vice with the best edge uppermost and the prepared face outward, remove the rough from the edge with a jack plane, finish with a trying plane, testing for straightness and

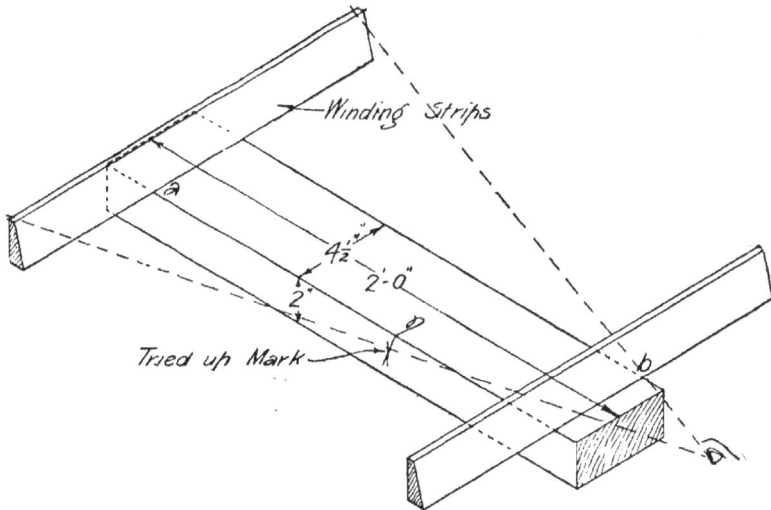

FIG. 77.

squareness with a straight-edge and try-square. Make a black-lead mark on the face side and face edge thus prepared, for purposes of identification; this is termed the tried-up mark.

Take a marking gauge and set to the required width—say $4\frac{1}{4}$ inches—and mark the face of the stuff, working the fence of the gauge against the face edge. Remove the surplus stuff to the gauge line, finishing with a trying plane and testing for squareness with the try-square. Reset the gauge to the required thickness—say $1\frac{7}{8}$ inches—mark the two shot edges, working the fence of the gauge against the face. Remove surplus stuff with a jack plane, finishing with the trying plane.

Preparing a Straight-edge. — Take a piece of

American yellow pine, 4 feet long, 3¼ inches wide, and ¾ inch thick, perfectly flat, straight grained, without sap, knots, or shakes.

Take rough off the wide faces and shoot a selected edge. Test if quite straight in the following manner :— Place straight-edge on a clean flat board as in Fig. 79, and press with black-lead pencil against edge to mark on board the outline of shot edge, as shown in dotted lines in Fig. 79, then turn piece over and mark outline of edge as before. If perfectly straight, both markings will coincide ; if not, the error will be exaggerated. If there be any error, shoot off where required till edge is perfectly straight.

It must be carefully noticed in marking outline of edge on board, that the piece must not be turned end for end, as it would be quite possible, in some instances, for edge outlines marked in that manner to coincide, and yet not be straight, as in Fig. 80.

Taper the width from the centre to the two ends, as shown, so that the straight edge is easily identified.

Winding Strips.—Take a piece of straight grained hard wood, mahogany preferred, thoroughly seasoned and without a knot, 1 foot 6 inches long, 2 inches wide, and 1 inch thick.

Prepare the same with the jack and trying planes, making one wide face perfectly flat and one edge straight, and place tried-up mark. Take to width and thickness of 1⅞ inches and ⅞ inch respectively, as previously described. Alter the gauge to ¼ inch, and mark the opposite edges from the opposite faces. Join the gauged lines at the ends with pencil lines, as shown in Fig. 81. Cut down carefully with the hand saw and plane the rough off the sawn faces. The wide faces may be smoothed with the smoothing plane, but edges must not be planed after being shot.

Jointing up of wide surfaces.—Boards are joined together at their edges for the purpose of forming wide surfaces ; the operations are as follows :—

The wide surfaces are at first planed, the boards are arranged to have the heart side and the outside of the boards alternating on any one face, as shown at A, Fig. 89, and not as shown at B. The heart side of a board always tends to become rounded ; the defects arising from this are minimised by the A

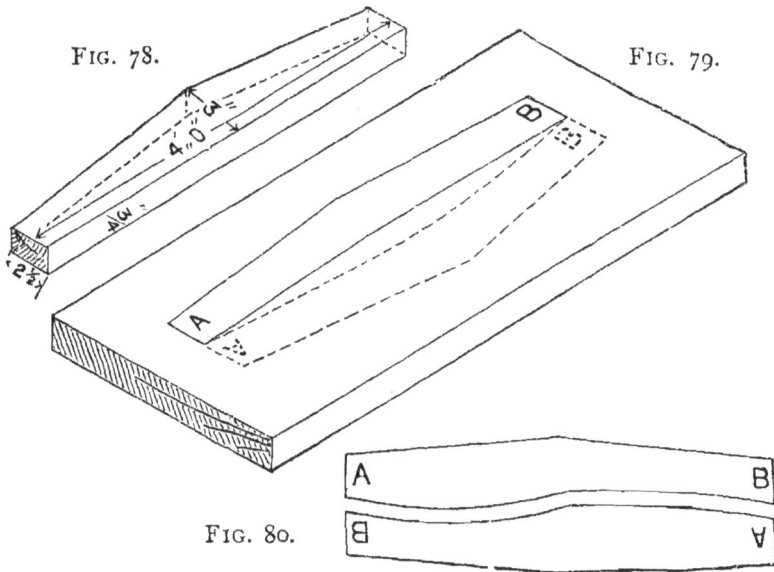

FIG. 78.   FIG. 79.

FIG. 80.

arrangement.   The edges are then shot, so that when placed in contact the joint is invisible.

The joints are of three kinds—the square, shown in Fig. 83 ; the cross-tongued joint, shown in Fig. 84 ; the dowelled joint, as shown in Fig. 85. For the first, the edges are shot. For the second, the edges are shot and grooved with a plough, the tongues are fitted ; these consist of strips of pine $\frac{1}{8}$ inch in thickness cut transversely to the length of the board by a cutting gauge as shown in Fig. 88. For the third, the edges are shot, then placed in contact, the position of the dowels is marked and then bored, and the dowels, which consist of small pieces of hard wood circular in section, are fitted. '

In glueing up the square joint one board is fixed in the bench vice, with the shot edge uppermost. The two jointed edges are placed side by side ; the glue is then applied with a brush. The boards are then placed in position with their edges in contact, and the upper board being rubbed backwards and

DIMENSION LINE

SHOWING GAUGE LINE

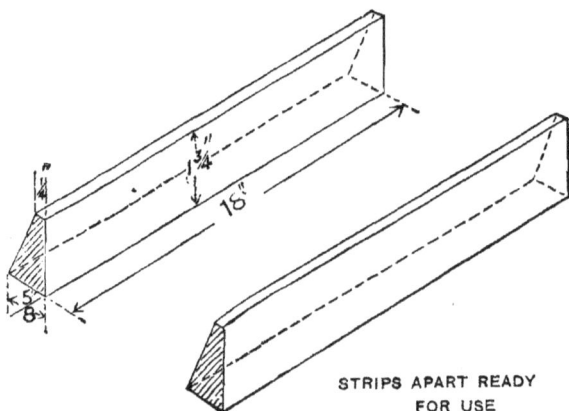

FIG. 81.

STRIPS APART READY FOR USE

FIG. 82.

forwards to work out all superfluous glue. If the boards are long it is usual to temporarily hold them together with cleats and dogs, as shown in Fig. 86. In glueing up the tongued joints the boards are placed in contact as before, the tongues are removed, and the grooves are filled with a wooden glue-spoon, as shown in Fig. 87 ; the tongues are inserted, and the glue applied to the remainder of the joint. The boards are then rubbed, cleated, and dogged, as before. In glueing up the dowelled joint no rubbing is possible ; the edges are therefore glued, placed in contact, and cleated and dogged as before. Where short or thin boards are to be jointed the operation of preparing the edges is carried out on a shooting board, as such boards can be held more rigidly in this position

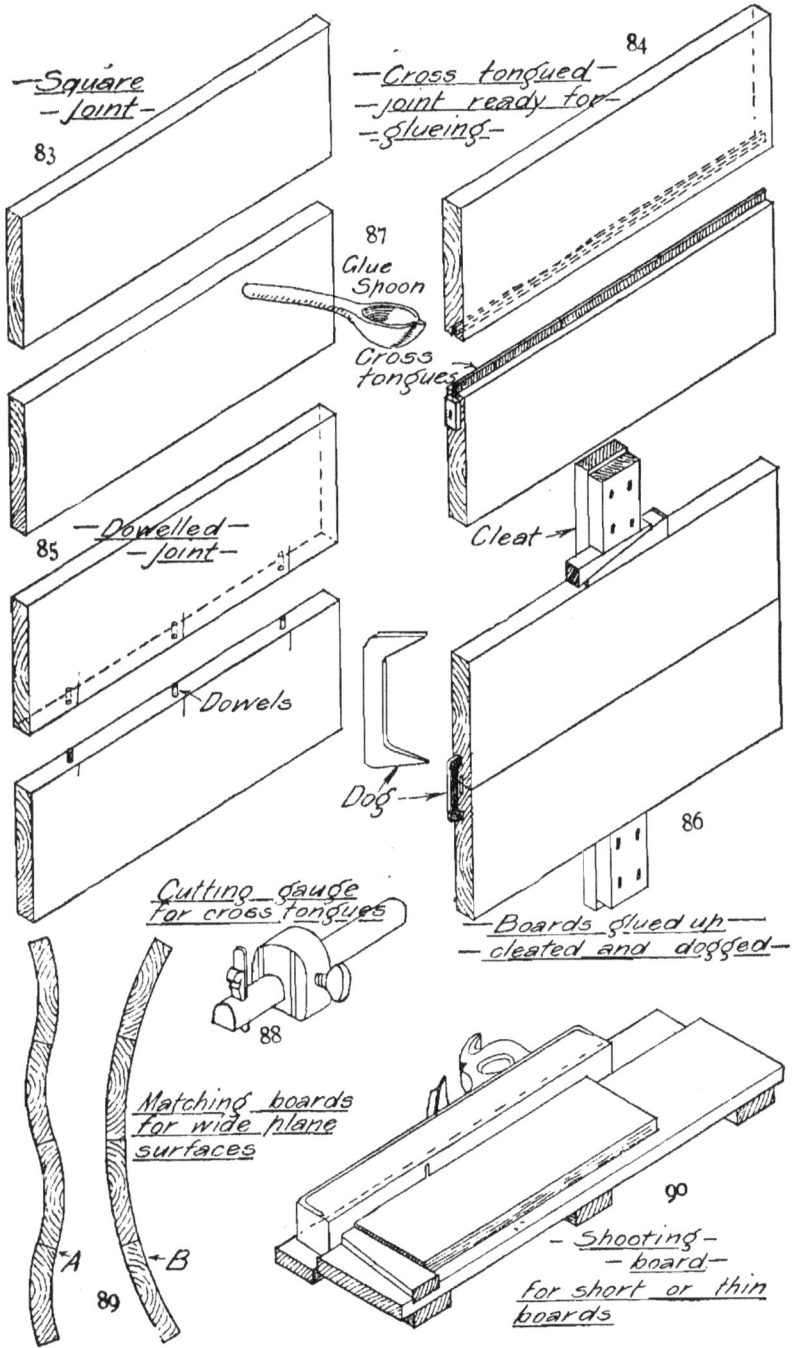

- Square Joint -

83

84

- Cross tongued -
- joint ready for -
- glueing -

87
Glue Spoon

Cross tongues

- Dowelled -
- joint -

85

Cleat →

↑ Dowels

Dog →

86

Cutting gauge
for cross tongues

88

- Boards glued up -
- cleated and dogged -

Matching boards
for wide plane
surfaces

90

← A   ← B

89

- Shooting -
- board -
for short or thin
boards

FIGS. 83 TO 90.—JOINTING-UP WIDE SURFACES.

than in a bench vice. Fig. 90 shows a shooting
board with trying plane and piece to be jointed in
this position.

Matchboarding.—Where wide surfaces are to be
covered with boards in positions where free expansion
and contraction is not possible, the boards have

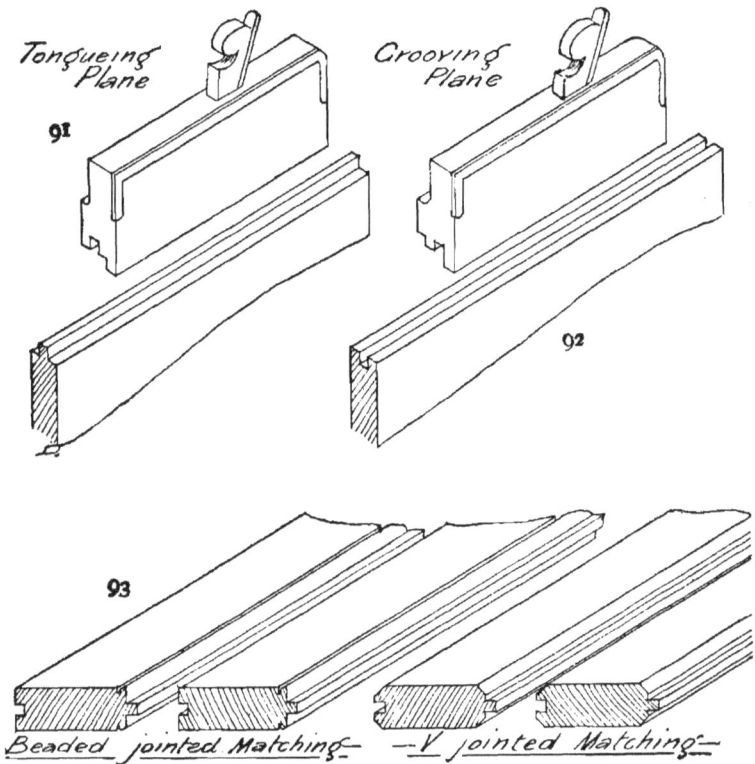

FIGS. 91 TO 93.—PREPARATION OF MATCH BOARDING.

grooves and tongues worked upon their jointed edges
to prevent an open through-joint in case of shrinkage.
The edges are not glued. The grooves and tongues
are worked by a special pair of planes known
as matching planes, as shown in Figs. 91 and 92.
The edges of the joint are usually moulded.
Beads or chamfers are the usual mouldings employed
for this purpose, as shown in Fig. 93.

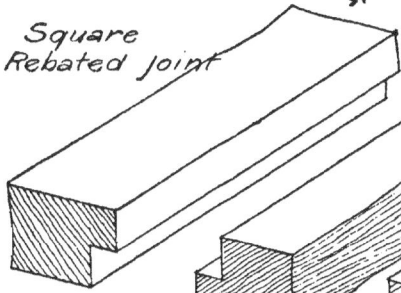

Square
Rebated joint

94

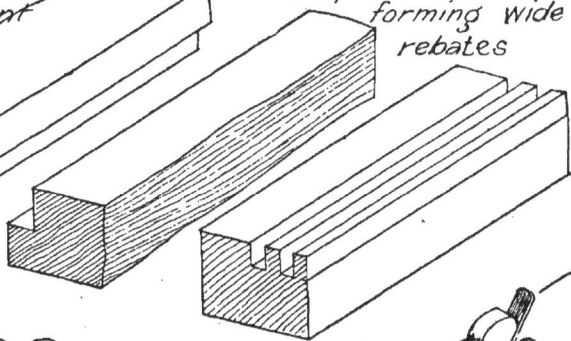

95

Plough grooves
preparatory to
forming wide
rebates

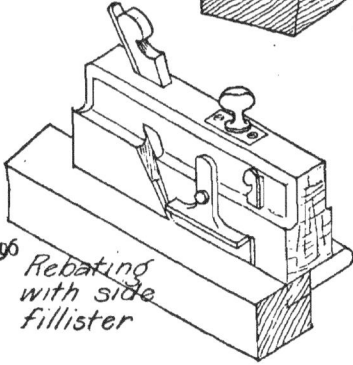

96 Rebating
with side
fillister

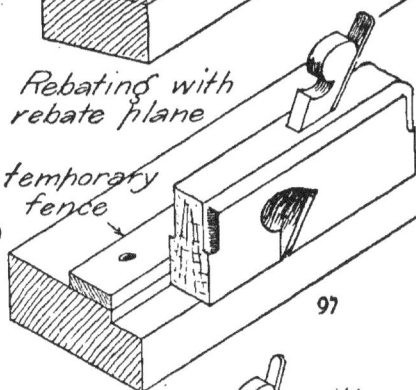

Rebating with
rebate plane

temporary
fence

97

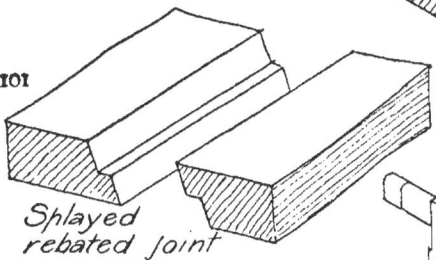

101

Splayed
rebated joint

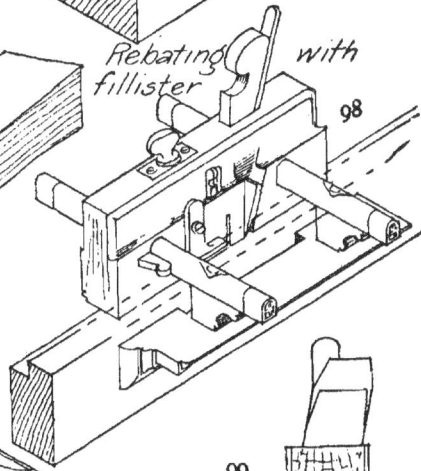

Rebating with
fillister

98

100

Badger Plane
for cleaning
wide rebates

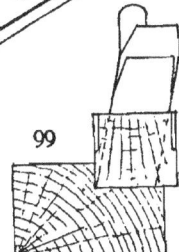

99

forming wide
rebate

FIGS. 94 TO 101.—REBATING.

Rebating.—This consists in forming a rectangular sinking in the edge of a piece of stuff, as shown in Fig. 94. Rebates are usually worked by one of the following four methods :—First, up to about 1½ inch in width by ¾ inch in depth, by means of a side fillister, as shown in Fig. 96. This tool has an adjustable fence and stop to regulate the width and depth respectively ; also a vertical cutter, that works in advance of the cutting-iron to ensure a sharp arris.

Similar size rebates may be worked with a rebate plane as shown in Fig. 97. A temporary fence is nailed on the surface of the stuff to regulate the width ; the depth is marked by a gauge.

Rebates up to 1 inch by 1 inch on the back edges of stuff are usually worked by a fillister, as shown in Fig. 98. The adjustable fence of this fillister differs from that of the side-fillister, but in other respects it is similar. Rebates wider than 1½ inch are worked as follows :—A series of grooves are worked in the stuff by means of a plough to the required depth of the rebate, as shown in Fig. 95 ; the stuff not removed by a plough is cleared out with a chisel, and the rebate is cleaned with a badger plane, as shown in Fig. 99. A badger plane is shown in Fig. 100; this is in many respects similar to a jack plane, but has the iron inserted on the skew, so that a shaving may be taken out up to the side of the plane. Rebated joints in doors or sashes that are required to fit very closely are made with splayed joints, as shown in Fig. 101.

Housing.—This is the term given to the sinking of the edge of one piece of stuff into another. There are three kinds. Fig. 104 is known as the plain housing ; it has the whole of the edge sunk into the side of the second member. Fig. 103 shows the shouldered housing ; this is employed where the two sunk members are required to be kept an exact distance apart. Fig. 102 shows the dovetailed housing ; this is employed where neither nails nor screws can be used. There are two methods of forming housings.

First, where the housing is required across the entire width of a member. A temporary fence is nailed, and the sinking formed with a grooving plane,

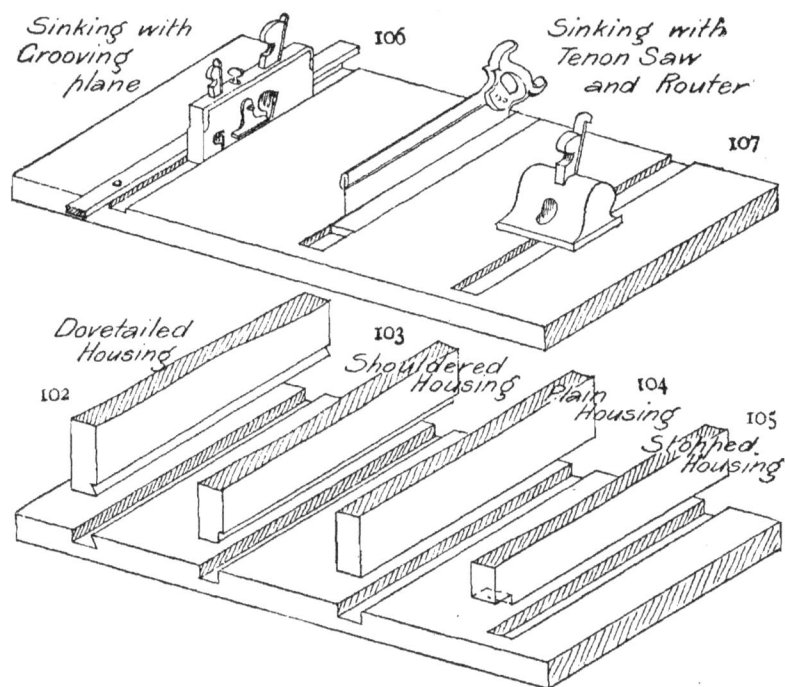

FIGS. 102 TO 107.—METHODS OF FORMING HOUSED JOINTS.

as shown in Fig. 106. These planes are made in various widths and each provided with a stop to regulate the depth of the sinking, and with two cutters in advance of the plane-iron to form sharp arrises.

Secondly, where the housing is stopped. A small portion of the housing at the stopped end is sunk with a chisel, the sides of the housing are cut with a tenon saw, the bulk of the material is removed with the chisel, and the sinking taken to the exact depth by means of the router, as shown in Fig. 107.

Chamfering.—If a triangular section is removed from the edge of a member, the resulting surface is termed a chamfer ; it is usually worked to an angle of 45° to the face. If the chamfer be taken from end to end of a piece of stuff it is usually worked with the ordinary bench planes ; but if it be stopped it is more convenient to use the chamfer plane shown in Figs. 108 and 109, which allows the chamfer to be worked to within ⅛ inch of the stop. There are several forms of stops, three of which are shown in Figs. 110, 112, and 113—the plain, the moulded, and the broached stops. The plain and moulded stops are expeditiously formed by cutting to a templet worked to the shape of the stop, as shown in Fig. 111. The broach stop, of which there are several kinds, must be carved.

Mouldings.—Mouldings may be worked by moulding planes the reverse of the moulding or by means of the plough and hollows and rounds. If the mouldings are small or there is a great quantity required, it is better to make a special plane ; if the mouldings are very large, or only a small quantity wanted, as much of the surplus material as possible should be removed with the plough, the finished section being worked with hollows and rounds, as shown in Figs. 114 and 115.

To ensure mouldings being cleanly worked, select the wood slightly cross-grained, as shown in Fig. 115A, and work that way of the edge running in the direction with the grain. This will prevent the tearing up of the surface, which is bound to occur if the grain is either curly or in the wrong direction, as all moulding planes have single irons only.

Bending.—The bending of wooden members is usually performed in one of five ways—(1) kerfing, (2)

108

Templet for
cutting stops

111

Stop Chamfer
Plane

Wedge

Iron

109

Adjustable
Block

Section through Stop
Chamfer Plane

Adjustable
Block

End View
of Plane

Plain
Stop

110

Moulded
Stop

112

Broach
Stop

113

115A

Section showing plough
grooves preparatory to
forming finished surfaces

Finished Section

114

115

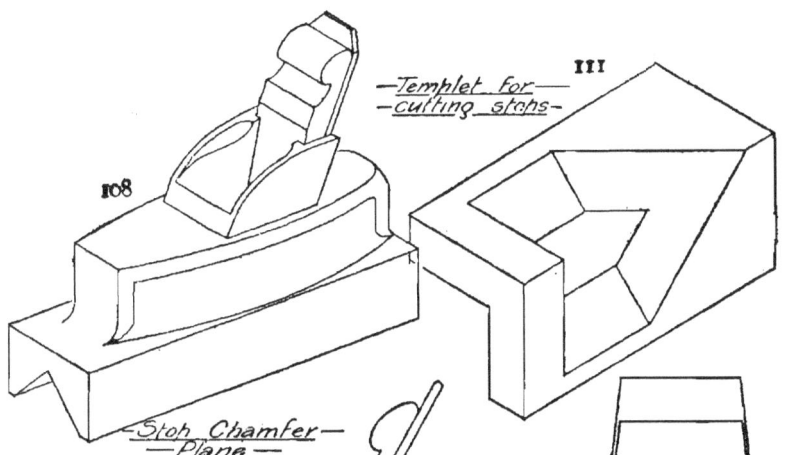

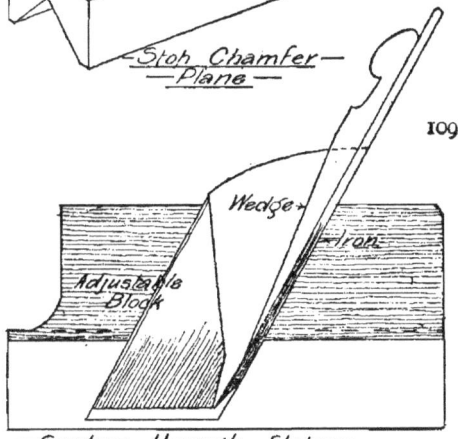

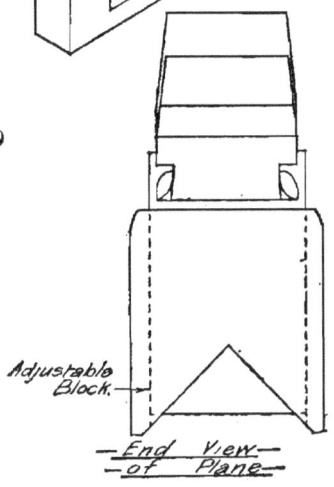

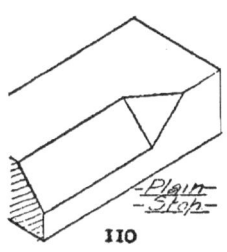

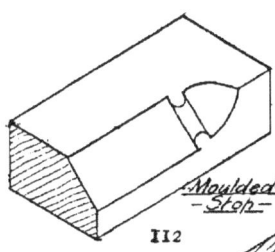

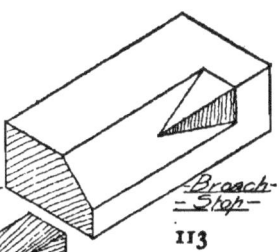

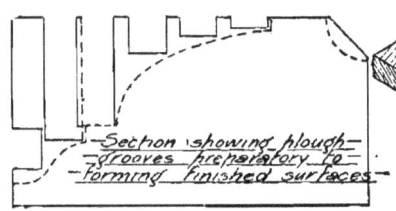

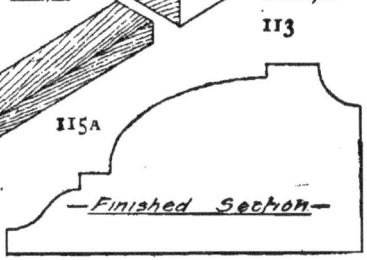

FIGS. 108 TO 115A.—CHAMFERING AND MOULDING.

building up, (3) stave and veneer method, (4) cooper-jointed method, (5) blocking and bending.

(1) The method of kerfing consists in making a series of transverse saw-cuts through the piece to be bent to within $\frac{1}{16}$ inch from the finished face. The face should be well damped ; the piece may then be bent to a curve, the quickness of which depends upon the thickness and frequency of the saw-cuts. If the required surface is concave the saw-cuts open when the piece is bent, feather-edge slips are fitted in the saw-cuts, and glued as shown in Fig. 116. If a convex surface is wanted the face is damped, the saw-cuts are filled with glue, and the piece is bent to fit a shaped bearer, which is screwed to the back, as shown in Fig. 117. Kerfing is an inferior method of bending, the position of the saw-cuts being in most cases discernible on the finished surfaces.

(2) The surfaces forming the method of building up are constructed of a series of narrow members cut to the curve required, and built and bonded similar to masonry, as shown in Fig. 118, and glued together. These surfaces when cleaned off form a sufficiently smooth ground for a painted surface. If a polished surface is required it will be necessary to veneer the surfaces in order to hide the numerous joints, and show a continuous grain.

(3) Sharp, concave curves are usually built up by the stave and veneer method. For this a cylinder is required to give the necessary form to the veneer, and is constructed as shown in Fig. 121. The veneer, which is well damped or steamed, is bent round the cylindrical surface, and is kept in position by pieces of stuff covering its extremities and screwed to the cylinder, as shown in Fig. 121. The staves, consisting of pieces of stuff 1 inch wide, $1\frac{1}{2}$ inches in thickness, are fitted to the cylinder and each other, and glued up ; when the glue is dry they are cleaned off at the back, and canvas is glued over the whole

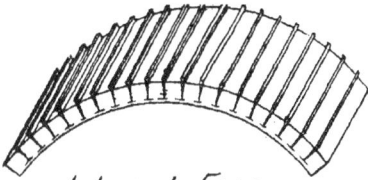

116

Internal Face
Saw Kerfs and feathers

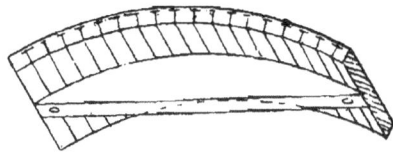

117

External face
Saw kerf and
shaped bearer

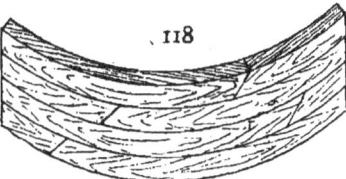

118

Built up Surface
for painted finish

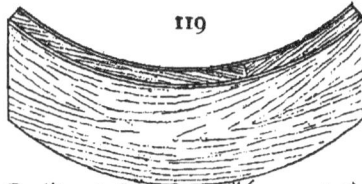

119

Built up Surface Veneered
for Polished finish

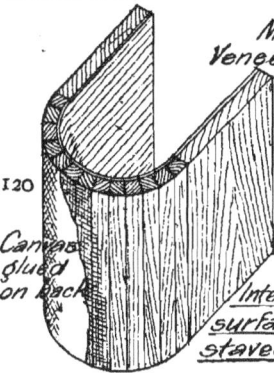

120

Canvas
glued
on back

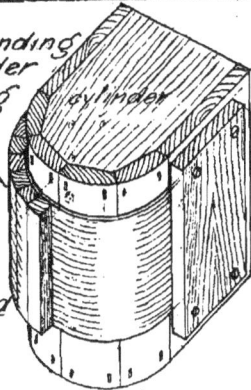

Method of bending
Veneer on cylinder
and fitting
staves

cylinder

121

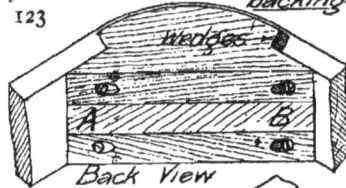

Internal Veneered
surface with
staved backing

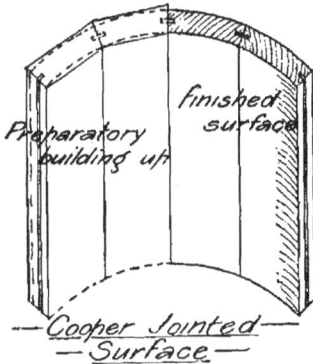

Preparatory
building up

finished
surface

Cooper Jointed
Surface

122

External angle with solid
backing

123

wedges

A   B

Back View

Front View

124

FIGS. 116 TO 124.—METHODS OF FORMING CURVED WOOD SURFACES.

F

surface to generally assist in binding the staves together, as shown in Fig. 120. The screws are then
withdrawn from the cylinder, the work removed and
cleaned up, as shown in Fig. 120.

(4) Cooper-jointing, as shown in Fig. 122, consists
in glueing up a series of narrow boards usually with
a tongued joint; when dry a templet to the curve
required is laid on each end and marked, and the
superfluous stuff is cleaned off. This method is
largely employed for panels and wood columns.

(5) Blocking and bending.—The piece of stuff to
be bent is sunk from the back surface to within $\frac{1}{16}$ inch
from the front face, a block is built up and cut to
the required shape, and the extremity A is screwed
to the first member, as shown in Fig. 123. The
veneered portion of the first member is then thoroughly
damped, and the contact surfaces of the veneer
and the block are then glued, the veneer is bent
round the block, wedges are inserted as shown to
draw the veneer tightly about the block, then screws
are inserted as shown at B. Fig. 124 shows a front
view.

Veneering.—Stuff—that is, wood used by the joiner
—is termed veneer when it is cut into thin sheets,
usually not exceeding $\frac{1}{16}$ inch in thickness ; it is generally prepared from rare or costly woods possessing a
beautiful colour or grain. It is used to enhance the
appearance of ornamental woodwork by covering
some or all of its visible parts with a layer of a more
strikingly marked piece of similar or other wood.
Veneer may be laid on work in large sheets, or it may
be cut into shaped pieces and laid to various designs.
For the latter purpose veneers of different woods are
often used in combination, and veneers may be dyed
several different colours to obtain any desired effect.

To veneer a piece of stuff, the following processes
in the order here given are usually carried out. First,
the board to be veneered, after having been planed

up, is traversed with a toothing plane, to remove any inequalities and to render the surface in a better condition to receive the glue.

The toothing plane has a stock similar to that of a smoothing plane ; it has a single-iron pitched vertically. The face of the iron is grooved with a number of small grooves parallel to its side, so that when the iron is sharpened from the back, as in the ordinary plane iron, the edge produced has a number of teeth.

If the board to be veneered is cut tangentially, the heart side should be chosen to be covered, in order that the natural tendency for the annual rings to straighten may always tend to keep the veneer taut. After having been toothed, the surface should be sized, to render it less porous, and at the same time the reverse side should be damped, to prevent the board from casting. The next process is to match and joint the pieces of the veneer on a board. They are temporarily secured in position to the surface with needle points. Strips of paper are then taken (damped on their upper sides and glued on the other) and laid on the veneer over the joints. The paper, on drying, draws the pieces close together and makes neat joints. In fixing the veneer, the board should be covered plentifully with glue of a medium consistency. There are two methods of securing the veneer—(1) with a caul hammer, (2) with a caul. The caul hammer is used on flat plane surfaces, where the veneer is in one piece and no tendency to crumble. After the board has been glued, the veneer is laid in position, its upper surface wetted, a hot flat iron is rapidly passed over the wetted upper surface to soften the glue, which is squeezed out by dragging the caul hammer over the upper surface, commencing at the centre and working diagonally towards the edges to ensure all air blisters and superfluous glue being worked out.

The caul hammer, as shown in Fig. 125, is a tool similar to a rake, but having a horizontal piece of iron about 4 inches in length and ¼ inch thick, with an edge straight in length and rounded transversely.

FIG. 125.

If the veneer is jointed to any pattern, or is of a crumbling nature, or is glued on a curved surface, it is usual to press it into position with a caul, which is removed when the glue has dried. The caul consists of a piece of stuff cut to the reverse of the surface to be veneered, or if it is a flat, plain surface, the caul is formed of boards, jointed to the dimension of the work to be veneered, so that when fixed the whole of the veneer is subjected to pressure. In the latter case cambered stretchers are employed to ensure the pressure being applied at the centre of the surface before the edges. Before applying the caul, it is heated to keep the glue in a melted condition while the caul is being fixed. Paper should be placed between the upper surface of the veneer and the caul, which latter should be well rubbed with soap to prevent the glue coming through the veneer and adhering to the caul. On wide surfaces in important work it is usual to veneer both sides of the work, because the veneer, in drying, contracts, and causes the surface on which it is glued to cast ; but if the stuff be veneered on both sides the opposing tendencies preserve a true surface.

Figs. 126 to 132 show the methods of veneering the parts of a small table, the construction of which is given on page 108. The rim is veneered by the arrangement known as feathering with narrow bands

of other coloured woods let in, leaving a narrow margin
about the edge. The process is as follows :—The veneer
for the groundwork for each of the four divisions
between the legs is feathered—that is, it is cut into
four pieces matched so that the grain forms a diamond
pattern, as shown in Fig. 126. The joints are shot
with a shoulder plane on a shooting board, and jointed
with paper, as before described. When dry, and
the ground and caul prepared, the former is glued
and the veneer laid on and the caul fixed in position,
as shown in Fig. 127. When dry the narrow margins
which for straight work are made to a variety of
patterns and can be bought ready made, are let in.
The ground to receive them is sunk by means of
a gauge with a cutter, as shown in Fig. 129, working
from the edges of the rim, the transverse cuts being
made with a knife and square. The ground is cleared
out, the narrow band is mitred, let in, glued, and
rubbed down with the back edge of the bench hammer,
and if necessary the caul is again applied. For the
circular top let it be assumed that the arrangement
is as follows :—The large central portion is covered
with four pieces of mahogany, feathered as before;
the outer rim is formed of eight or more pieces, also
of mahogany, made so that its grain radiates to the
centre as nearly as possible. The intermediate bands
are formed of (1) an ebony line, (2) a boxwood line,
(3) an ebony line, (4) a satin wood band $\frac{1}{2}$ inch wide,
then with ebony and boxwood alternating, as before.
Then the process would be as follows: The large
feathered ground would be jointed ; the top would be
prepared by toothing, and the position of the joints
on the veneer set out on its surface and edges. The
top is glued and the veneer applied, making its joints
coincide with the positions previously set out. To
retain the veneer in position, two or three veneer
pins should now be placed near to the edge of the
veneer, leaving them projecting about $\frac{1}{8}$ inch for the

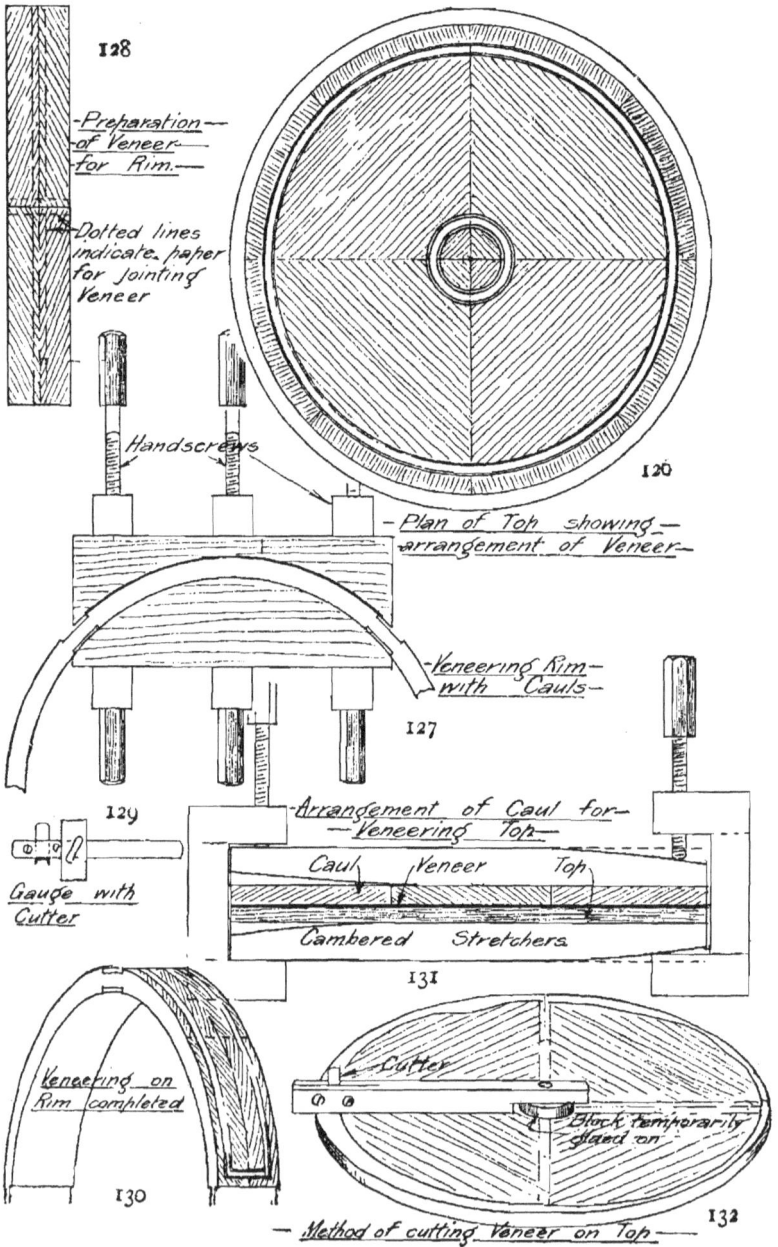

128

-Preparation-
-of Veneer-
-for Rim.-

-Dotted lines
indicate paper
for jointing
Veneer

Handscrews

120

-Plan of Top showing-
-arrangement of Veneer-

-Veneering Rim
with Cauls-

127

129

-Arrangement of Caul for-
-Veneering Top-

Gauge with
Cutter

Caul   Veneer   Top

Cambered   Stretchers

131

Veneering on
Rim completed

130

Cutter

Block temporarily
glued on

- Method of cutting Veneer on Top -

132

FIGS. 126 TO 132.—METHODS OF VENEERING PARTS OF TABLE.

purpose of withdrawal. A caul would be prepared of slightly larger dimensions than the top, and heated and placed over the veneer; then cambered stretchers in pairs would be fixed with handscrews, as shown in Fig. 131, about 6 to 9 inches apart; when the glue is dry the caul would be removed, a small block would be temporarily glued in the centre, as shown in Fig. 132, to which the radius rod for cutting is fixed ; the outer edge of the ground would then be cut circular, as indicated in Fig. 132. The outer band would now be matched, jointed, and glued. When dry, the space for the intermediate bands would be cut out with a cutter to the exact width of the complete band ; the satin wood would then be fixed in pieces, the grain radiating to the centre, and then glued. When dry the spaces for the ebony and box-wood lines would be cut out, and the lines which are narrow enough to bend about the curve can be jointed, glued, and rubbed in with the edge of a bench hammer. When all is dry it is cleaned off with a fine toothing plane if necessary, finally with a scraper and glass-paper.

JOINTS

Mortise and Tenon Joints.—The joints for framing are usually one or other of the forms of mortise and tenon joints. Figs. 133 to 140 show types for different purposes. The parts of a mortise and tenon joint are as follows :—The tenon, haunchion, shoulder, and the mortise, as shown in Fig 133. The thickness of the tenon should be such that the substance should be sufficient to resist crushing under the pressure of the wedge, and the width must be reduced to a dimension that the shrinkage shall be inappreciable. The thickness of single tenons is usually made one-third the thickness of the frame, and the width up to five times the thickness to a maximum of two inches, as shown in Fig. 135. The combined thickness of the tenons for double tenons, as shown in Fig. 134, should be equal to one-third the thickness of the frame. The haunchion is a shortened portion of the tenon, usually $\frac{1}{2}$ inch in length, and its purpose is to strengthen the root of the tenon and to prevent the twisting of the rail. The shoulders should be cut square in order to obtain perfect contact with the mortised member of the frame. The mortise is a sinking made to receive the tenon of the abutting member ; it is made tapering outwards to receive the wedges with which the parts are held together, as shown in Fig. 133. Figure 136 shows the method of foxtail wedging employed where it is undesirable for the end grain of the tenon to be seen. Fig. 137 illustrates a barefaced tenon used wherever the tenoned rail is of a less thickness than the mortised member, as in the lower rail of a skylight. Fig. 138 shows the mortise and tenon for a moulded and rebated sash. In these the haunchion is usually

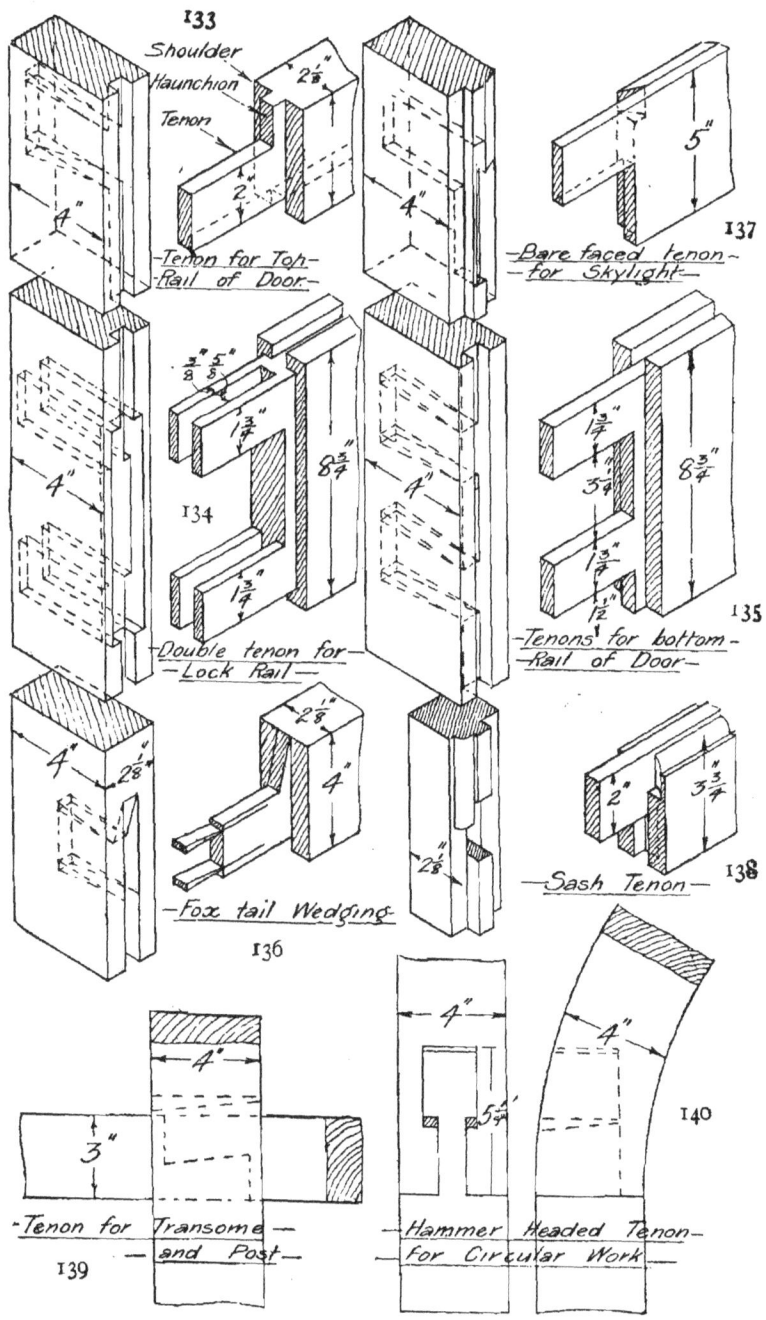

133

Shoulder

Haunchion

Tenon

$2\frac{1}{8}$"

2"

4"

-Tenon for Top-
-Rail of Door-

4"

137

5"

-Bare faced tenon-
-for Skylight-

4"

$\frac{3}{8}$" $\frac{5}{8}$"

$1\frac{3}{4}$"

$8\frac{3}{4}$"

134

$1\frac{3}{4}$"

-Double tenon for-
-Lock Rail-

4"

$1\frac{3}{4}$"

$\frac{3}{4}$"

$8\frac{3}{4}$"

$1\frac{3}{4}$"

$1\frac{1}{2}$"

135

-Tenons for bottom-
-Rail of Door-

4" $2\frac{1}{8}$"

$2\frac{1}{8}$"

4"

$2\frac{1}{8}$"

-Fox tail Wedging-

136

2" $3\frac{3}{4}$"

-Sash Tenon- **138**

4"

3"

-Tenon for Transome-
-and Post-

139

4"

4"

$5\frac{1}{4}$"

-Hammer Headed Tenon-
-For Circular Work-

140

FIGS. 133 TO 140.—MORTISE AND TENON JOINTS.

worked on the mortised member, and the moulding is scribed together at the joint. Fig. 139 shows the method of tenoning a transome to a post. In this instance the mortise is made slightly wider than the width of the transome ; the tenons of the two pieces of the transome are bevelled-halved together, and are wedged into their position by a pair of folding wedges. Fig. 140 illustrates the hammer-headed tenon employed in connecting two-curved or a straight and a curved member. In this at the extremity of the tenon there is a projection at each side to form an abutment for the wedges, which are inserted as shown.

Tusk Tenon.—This is employed to connect two beams of equal depth. To obtain the greatest depth under these conditions, the tenons should be placed in the neutral layer of the beam. The thickness of the tenon should be the depth divided by six, the haunchion should be sunk $\frac{1}{6}$ the breadth of the beam, and it should extend half-way from the underside of the tenon to the underside of the beam ; the tenon is secured by a wedge or key inserted in a mortise made through the tenon on the outer side of the mortised member. Figs. 141 and 142 illustrate this method.

Bridle Joint.—The bridle joint, as shown in Figs. 143 and 144, is employed in skew or inclined abutment members of carpentry work where it is desirable to get the maximum shearing area, as indicated by the dotted lines. It is the reverse of the ordinary mortise and tenon, as may be observed in the diagram. It is usually secured by an iron bolt.

Draw-boring.—This is a method chiefly used in carpentry work for securing mortise and tenon joints ; it was also used in mediæval joinery work, and also in modern reproductions. The mortise and tenon, as shown in Figs. 145 and 146, are first fitted, the hole to receive pin is bored through the mortised

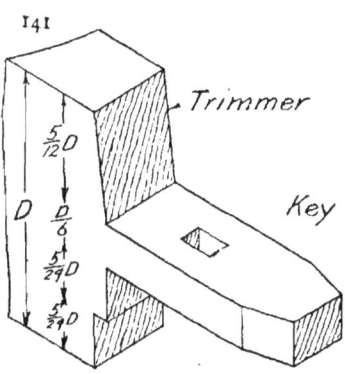

141

Trimmer

$\frac{5}{12}D$

D

$\frac{D}{6}$

$\frac{5}{24}D$

$\frac{3}{24}D$

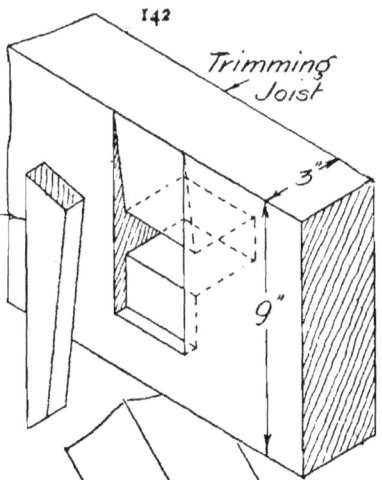

142

Trimming
Joist

Key

3″

9″

—Tusk Tenon—

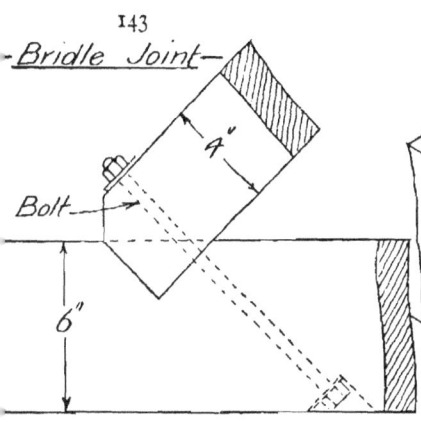

143
—Bridle Joint—

4″

Bolt

6″

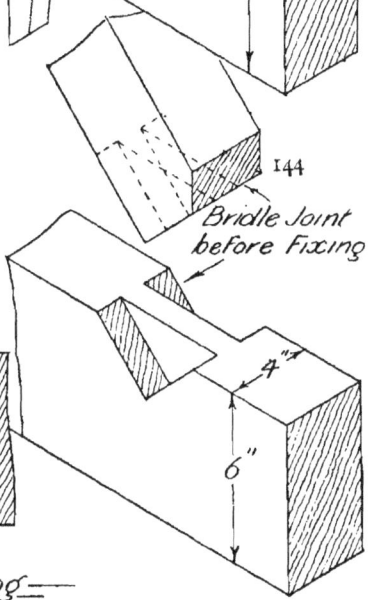

144

Bridle Joint
before Fixing

4″

6″

—Draw Boring—

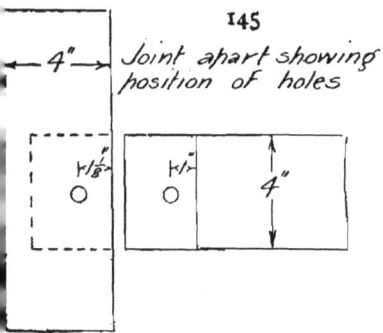

145
Joint apart showing
position of holes

4″

$\frac{1}{8}$″

$\frac{1}{-}$″

4″

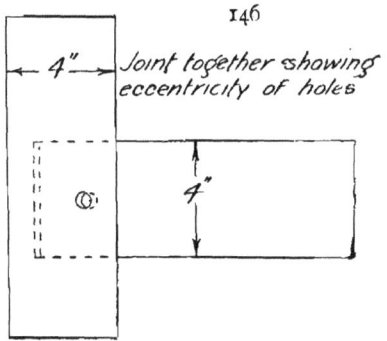

146
Joint together showing
eccentricity of holes

4″

4″

FIGS. 141 TO 146.—DRAW-BORING.

member ; the pieces are then put together, and the position of the hole marked on the tenon, after which the latter is withdrawn, and the hole is bored through the tenon slightly nearer the shoulder than the position marked. The members are then put together, and secured by a dowel made from oak or other tough wood. The eccentric boring has the effect of causing the shoulder and the abutting surface to come into close contact upon the dowel being driven through.

Dovetailing.—There are three general forms of dovetails—the plain, the lap, and the secret. The plain dovetail is usually employed for joining the angles of boxes, or any such work in which the appearance of the joint is not objectionable. It is important if wide surfaces are to be connected to dispose the length joints, as shown in Fig. 149, to ensure the parts being properly bonded. In boxes or similar work the pins and the dovetails should be nearly equal in dimensions. The lap dovetail, as shown in Fig. 150, is employed in connecting the fronts and sides of drawers, where the appearance of the end grain of the dovetails would be objectionable, and where the end grain of the pins is not visible when the parts are in position. The secret dovetail, as shown in Fig. 151, is used by cabinet-makers to connect the sides of small boxes or cabinets where any visible end grain would detract from the appearance of the work. If a number of similar parts are to be constructed, the members with the dovetails are connected together by handscrews, and the whole cut together, it being much easier to cut a number square and true than when cutting them singly, saves time in the setting out, and ensures a similarity in the work. The method of marking the pins is shown in Fig. 152. The dovetailed member is placed in position on the end grain of the member in which the pins are to be formed. The pins are then marked with a dovetailed saw, as shown.

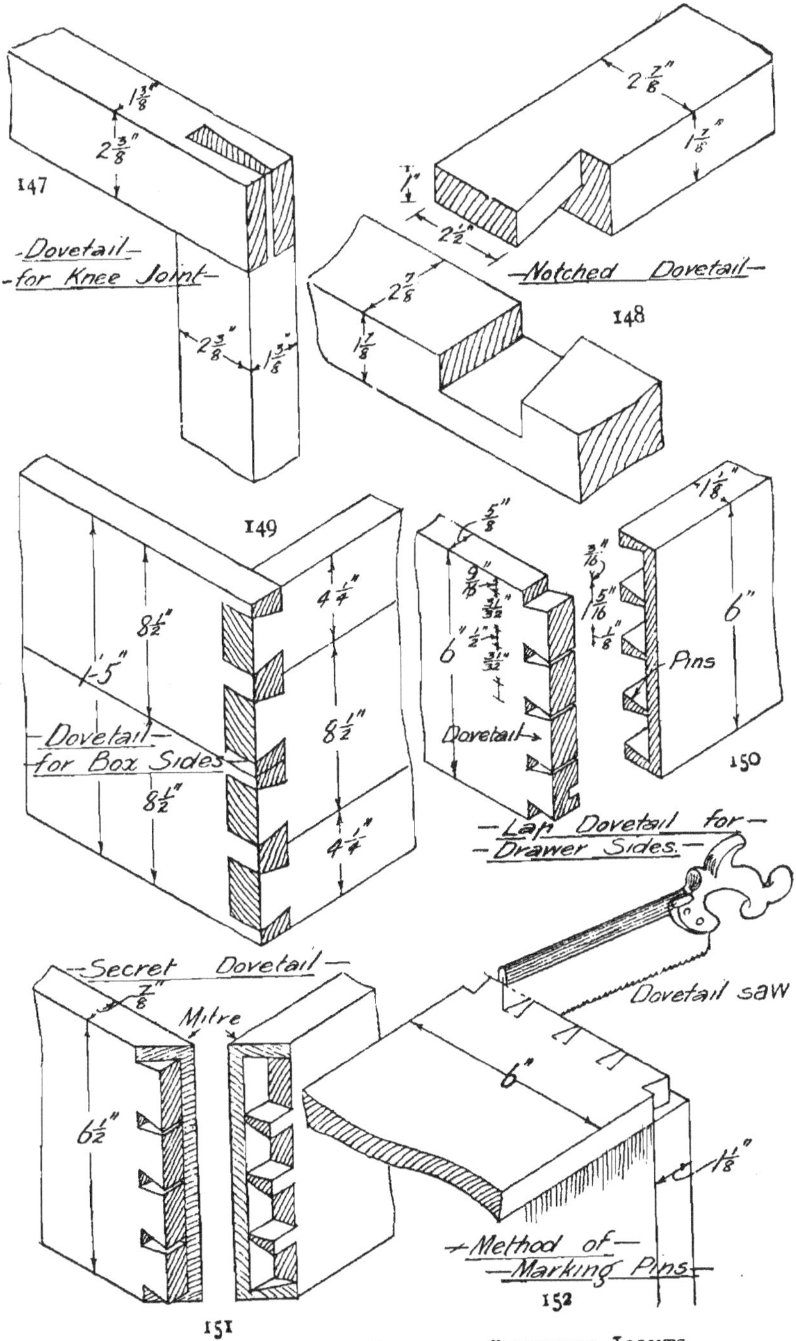

147

Dovetail
for Knee Joint

$1\frac{3}{8}''$

$2\frac{3}{8}''$

$2\frac{7}{8}''$

$1\frac{7}{8}''$

$\frac{1}{4}''$

$2\frac{1}{2}''$

Notched Dovetail

148

$2\frac{7}{8}''$

$1\frac{3}{8}''$

$2\frac{3}{8}''$ $1\frac{3}{8}''$

149

$4\frac{1}{4}''$

$8\frac{1}{2}''$

$1·5''$

Dovetail
for Box Sides

$8\frac{1}{2}''$

$8\frac{1}{2}''$

$4\frac{1}{4}''$

$\frac{5}{8}''$

$\frac{9}{16}''$

$\frac{3}{8}''$

$6''$

$\frac{1}{2}''$

$\frac{1}{4}''$

Dovetail

$\frac{3}{16}''$

$\frac{5}{16}''$

$\frac{1}{8}''$

$\frac{1}{8}''$

$6''$

Pins

150

Lap Dovetail for
Drawer Sides.

Secret Dovetail

$\frac{7}{8}''$

Mitre

$6\frac{1}{2}''$

Dovetail saw

$6''$

Method of
Marking Pins

$1\frac{1}{8}''$

151

152

FIGS. 147 TO 152.—FORMS OF DOVETAIL JOINTS.

With the secret dovetails it is necessary to cut the pins first, and then mark the mortices from them.

Fig. 147 shows the adaptation of the plain dovetail for a knee joint in quartering, and Fig. 148 shows a notched dovetail to connect two pieces of quartering at right angles to each other.

Angle Joints.—These are subdivided as follows :—

1. Those with joints parallel to the grain.

2. Those with joints at right angles to the grain.

3. Those in which the joints may be parallel or at right angles to the grain.

In all angle joints it is necessary for good work to have either a rebated or grooved and tongued joint. The rebated are the easier to form, but with these it is necessary to employ nails or screws to connect the joint ; where glue only is used it is necessary to have a groove and tongue.

Figs. 153 to 155 show joints parallel to the grain. Fig. 153 is a bead and rebate joint, put together without glue. In this case it is difficult to form a close joint ; the bead is therefore placed to detract from any defect. Fig. 154 is a similar joint put together with glue, therefore with a groove and tongue instead of with a rebate. Fig. 155 shows an angle bead and rebated joint, the angle here being emphasised by a large bead. Figs. 156 to 158 illustrate joints at right angles to the grain. The first of these is a plain mitre—an easy joint to fit, but difficult to fix, and weak ; the second, a mitred and tongued joint. A cross tongue is employed, which ensures the parts coming together properly and forms a strong joint. The third is a mitred and shouldered joint, used where one member is thicker than the other.

Figs. 159 to 161 show joints which may be used either parallel or perpendicular to the grain. The first shows a mitred and rebated joint, used where it is intended to fix the parts with nails or screws. Figs.

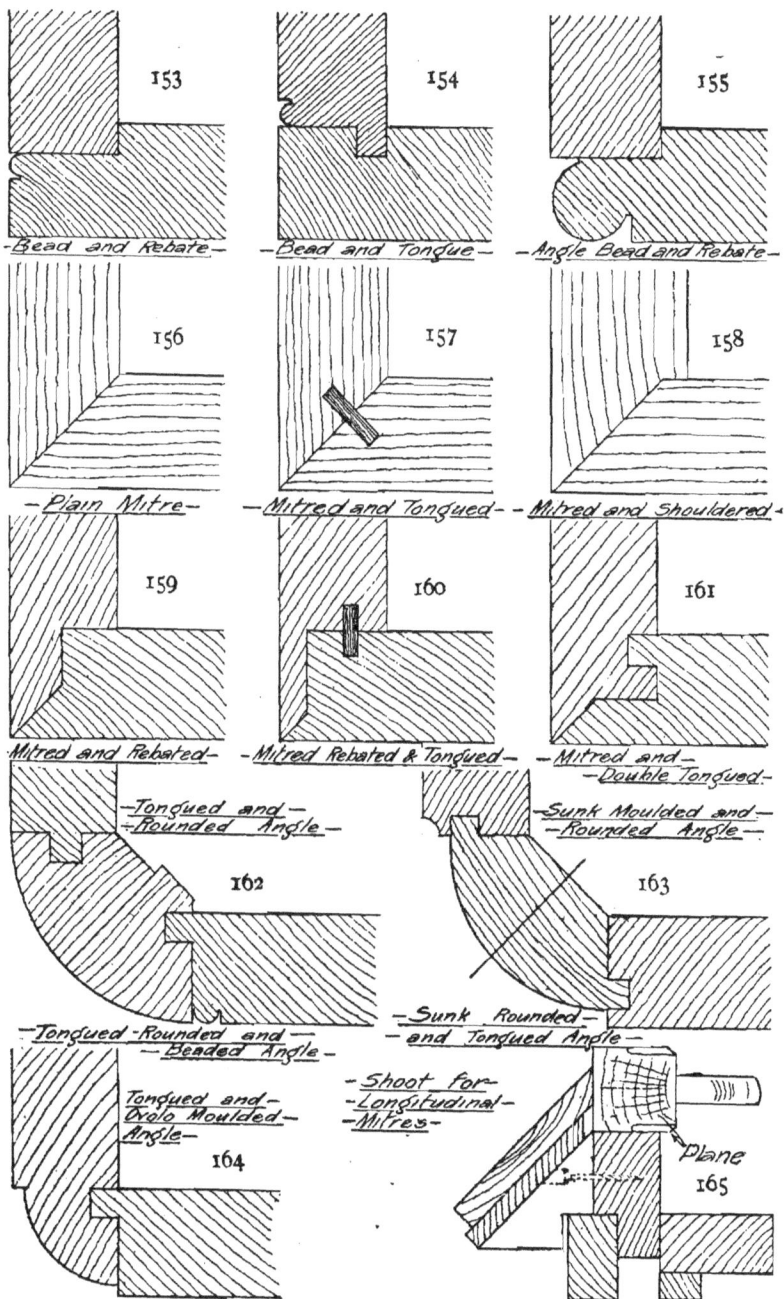

153 — Bead and Rebate —

154 — Bead and Tongue —

155 — Angle Bead and Rebate —

156 — Plain Mitre —

157 — Mitred and Tongued —

158 — Mitred and Shouldered —

159 Mitred and Rebated —

160 — Mitred Rebated & Tongued —

161 — Mitred and — Double Tongued —

— Tongued and — Rounded Angle —

162

— Sunk Moulded and — Rounded Angle —

163

— Tongued -Rounded and — Beaded Angle —

— Sunk Rounded — and Tongued Angle —

Tongued and — Ovolo Moulded — Angle —

164

— Shoot for — Longitudinal — Mitres —

Plane

165

FIGS. 153 TO 165.—ANGLE JOINTS.

160 and 161 are joints intended to be secured with glue only. Figs. 162 to 164 show special cases of joints with the grain. Fig. 162 is a method of forming a rounded corner either with a plain tongued joint, or with a tongued and beaded joint. Fig. 163 illustrates a sunk rounded angle. Fig. 164 shows a smaller rounded angle, which may be formed in the thickness of the stuff. Fig. 165 is a section of a shoot for forming long mitres.

Scarfed Joints.—Pieces of timber may be lengthened by one of the forms of scarfing joints. If the timbers are subjected to a compressional stress, the abutting surfaces should have a maximum area. Fig. 166 is the best form for this purpose ; Fig. 167 is a good form where it is necessary to have good heading joints, as the folding wedges indicated admit of the adjacent pieces being drawn tightly together. For tensional stresses Fig. 168 is the best form, as it gives the greatest strength at the root of the scarf. Fig. 169 is also a good form for the same purpose. For carpentry work these joints require fish plates to render them as strong as the uncut portion.

Bearing Joints.—Where it is required to have two timbers crossing they may be connected by the notched joint, in which case one timber is notched to fit over the adjoining member, one timber only being cut, as shown in Fig. 170. Where the two timbers are equally sunk, as shown in Fig. 171, the timbers are said to be halved.

Cogging.—Where the two members are cut and fitted together with a tooth or cog on one piece, and a corresponding sinking on the other, as shown in Fig. 172, they are said to be cogged.

Bevelled Halving.—Two timbers jointed at right angles to each other are often connected by the joint shown in Fig. 173, the advantage being that when nailed together the shoulder is drawn into close contact, and tends to remain in position.

170

2"

3"

2"

3"

—Notched Joint—

172

2"

3"

2"

3"

—Cogged Joint—

2"

3"

171

2"

3"

173

2"

3"

—Halved—
—Joint—

—Bevilled—
—Halved Joint—

—Halved Joint—

2"

3"

1'-0"

166

—Scarfed Joints—

2"

3"

1'-0"

167

2"

1"

1'-0"

168

2"

3"

1'-1"

169

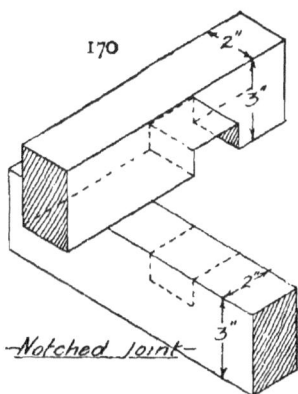

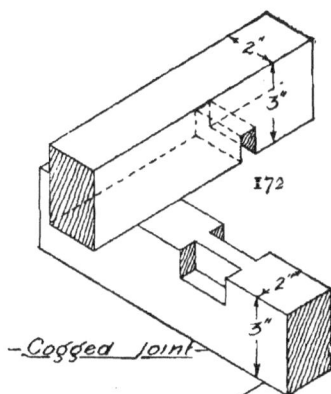

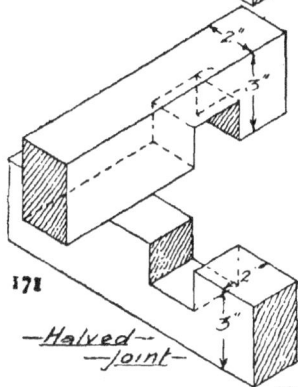

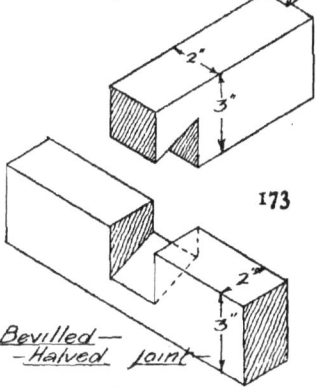

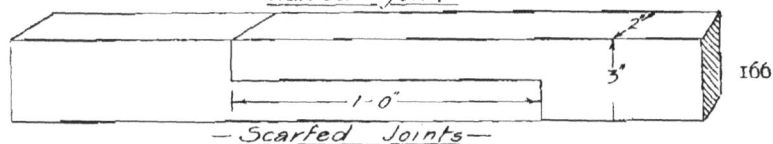

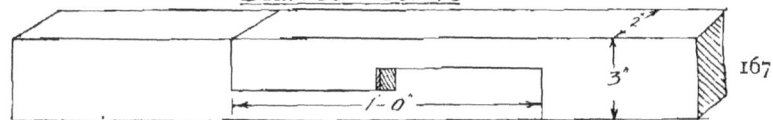

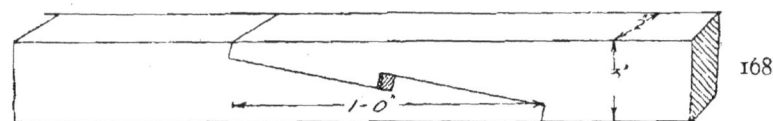

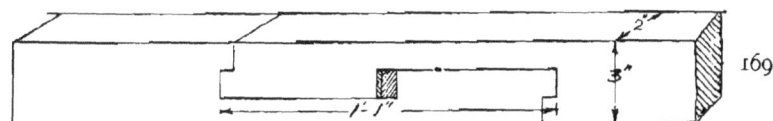

FIGS. 166 TO 173.—SCARFED JOINTS.

G

EXERCISES

THE following examples are taken to illustrate the processes and operations before described :—

Wall Bracket.—All stuff in joinery is usually cut from $\frac{1}{4}$ inch to 2 inches longer and $\frac{1}{4}$ inch wider than the finished dimensions, to allow for the dressing and working. Figs. 174 to 178 illustrate the construction of a wall bracket. Take three pieces of American pine, or any suitable wood, cut to the figured dimensions plus the allowance for dressing. Take out of winding, shoot edges, and thickness. Set out housings. First fit support to shelf with a dovetailed stopped housing, as shown in Fig. 178, house the shelf and support into the back with a stopped housing. Strike the shape of the shelf by means of a compass set to $5\frac{3}{8}$ inches radius. Prepare a pattern for the shape of the support and back. Prepare another pattern for half of the upper portion of the back ; this is symmetrical about a centre line, and therefore must be marked by reversing the pattern. Cut these shapes with the bow-saw, and finish them with the spokeshave, scraper, chisel, and glass-paper. Clean up the faces of the three pieces with a smoothing plane ; finish with glass-paper rubbed in the direction of the grain. Glue the dovetail on the support and the sinking to receive it in the shelf ; put together. Glue the housing in the back, fit in shelf and support, and fix by screwing from the back, as shown in Figs. 176 and 177. Clean any glue that may have been squeezed out of the joints with a clean rag, hot water, and chisel.

Picture Frame.—Take a piece of hard wood—say mahogany—4 feet long, $2\frac{1}{4}$ inches wide, 1 inch thick. Take out of winding, shoot one edge, gauge, and reduce to a width and thickness as dimensioned on Fig. 179.

With a fillister from the front face work a double rebate, as shown in Fig. 181, sinking that rebate which is more remote from the face first ; then with moulding planes work the two mouldings on the front face and clean with glass-paper. To ensure the

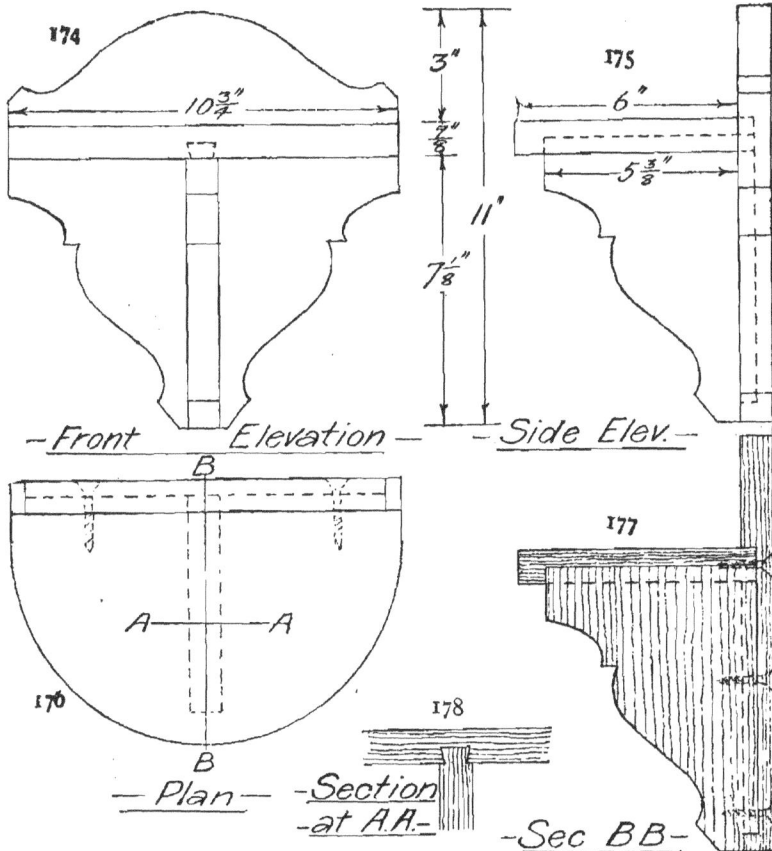

FIGS. 174 TO 178.—WALL BRACKET.

mouldings being cleanly worked, select the wood slightly cross-grained, as previously described in the section on mouldings. Cut all the lengths with their mitres in the order shown to ensure the abutting surfaces matching perfectly, as there is usually some want of uniformity in the section, especially when worked with hollows and rounds. Shoot all the mitres, and glue up the frame. It will be necessary to strengthen the glued mitres by keys, nails, or screws. The frame may be held together till the glue has dried with cords and blocks, as indicated in Fig. 182. A better method is to secure the angles with corner cramps, as shown in Fig. 185, which hold the stuff rigidly, and allow the supplementary fastenings to be added at once. The frame should be carefully bored before inserting nails or screws. Fig. 183 shows the method of forming a key. For this purpose two converging cuts are made with a coarsely-set saw; into these a piece of veneer is glued and inserted. This, when dry, forms a strong joint. Fig. 184 shows a dovetail key. For this purpose a piece of similar stuff to the frame is prepared slightly thinner on one edge than the other; a similar section is removed from the angle of the frame, slightly tapering in its length; the dovetail-shaped key, being slightly wedge-shaped in length, can be fitted exactly. When dry the frame is cleaned up, the glass is bedded in the rebate in a thin bed of white lead, or a slip of paper is pasted in the angle to make a dust-proof joint. The mount and picture are now inserted; the combined thickness of the glass, mount, and picture should be slightly greater than the depth of the first rebate. The pine back is now fitted and screwed into the frame ; after this, strips of brown paper should be glued over the joints between the back and the frame to ensure the enclosed space being dust-proof. Inferior frames, as shown in Fig. 180, have one rebate and the back secured by nails driven into the frame, as shown.

Tool Chest.—Take off the quantities of the material, preferably northern pine, making the usual allowances. Joint and glue up the sides, ends, and top, taking care to bond the joints on sides and ends as shown in Figs. 186 and 187 ; joint the stuff for bottom, and make matchboard joints. Fit and glue up the

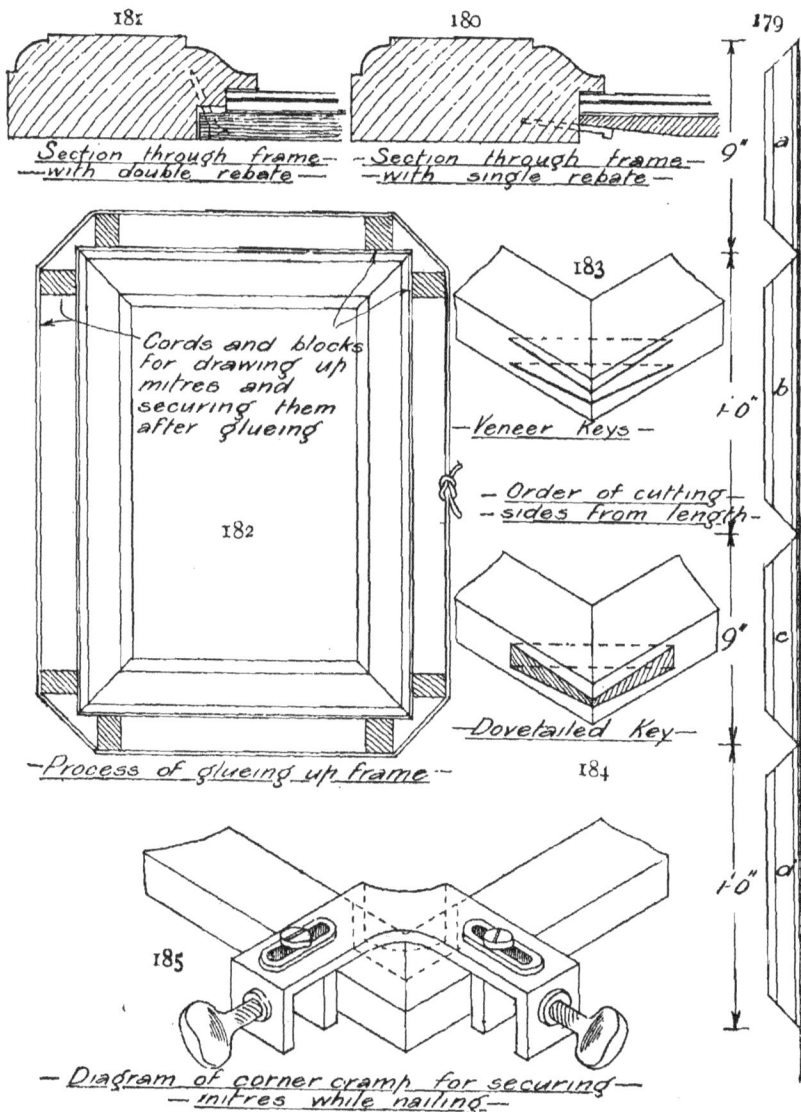

181

Section through frame
—with double rebate—

180

—Section through frame—
—with single rebate—

179

9″ a

183

—Veneer Keys—

Cords and blocks
for drawing up
mitres and
securing them
after glueing

182

— Order of cutting —
—sides from length—

1·0″ b

9″ c

—Dovetailed Key—

184

—Process of glueing up frame—

1·0″ d

185

— Diagram of corner cramp for securing—
—mitres while nailing—

FIGS. 179 TO 185.—MITREING OF FRAMES.

frame for lid ; prepare the plinth and lid rim.   Clean up the sides and top.   Dovetail and glue up the sides and ends ; when dry, level the top and bottom edges, test for squareness, and nail on temporary brace. Lay on bottom boards, and fix with screws.   Screw the lid frame to lid, and shoot edges to fit the box ; mitre the plinth about the base of the box, and fix with glue and nails ; mitre the rim about the lid, and fix with glue and nails ; mitre the string about the box, and fix with glue and nails.   Fit the lid so that it works easily into the rebate, and hang with butt hinges.   Prepare, fit and fix the side battens with screws.   Prepare stuff for trays, dovetailing the sides and ends, and fit on to bearers as shown in Fig. 188.   A perspective sketch of the chest is shown in Fig. 189.   Fit box lock in the centre of the front.

Housemaid's Box.—Take off quantities of the material, preferably American pine, making the usual allowances.   Make full size working and outline drawings, as shown in Figs. 190 to 195, and develop the true widths and shapes of sides and ends.   Determine the true bevel for the sloping edges of ends and sides in the manner shown in Fig. 195.   These edges are best shot on a shooting board set to the required inclination.   Place the sides together and cut the dovetails.   It might be noted that in cutting the dovetails they are not paired face to face, as the cuts are not made at right angles to the face, but parallel to the top and bottom edges.   The pins are marked in the usual manner, and cut parallel to the top and bottom edges.   Glue up the sides, screw on the bottom, fix bearers for tray.   The sides of the tray must be set out in a similar manner to the sides of the box, the divisions being housed in. Screw the iron handles on the sides.

Kitchen Table.—Figs 196 to 200 give working drawings of a small kitchen table.   Take off the

187

Side battens

3"

1'-6"

— Side Elevation —

188

½" Top· ½" Frame

Tray

Tray

⅞" Sides

1"×2" Bearer

Rim
String

— Transverse
Section —

⅝" Plinth.

186

3"

3"

8⅜"

⅞" Matched Bottom

— Half Longitudinal Section —

2¼"
2"

10¾"

1'-6"

3'-0"

3"

— Front Elevation —

— Half

— General Sketch — 189

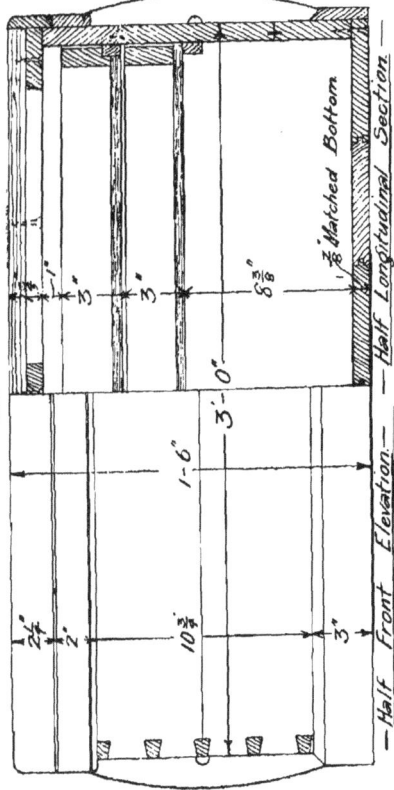

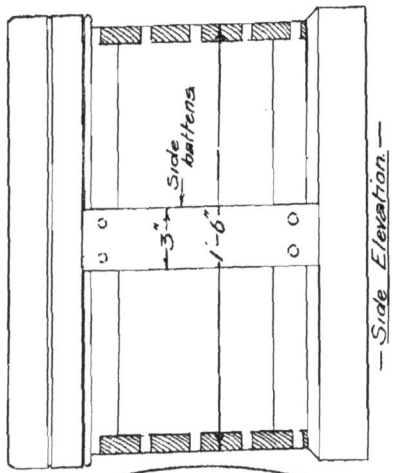

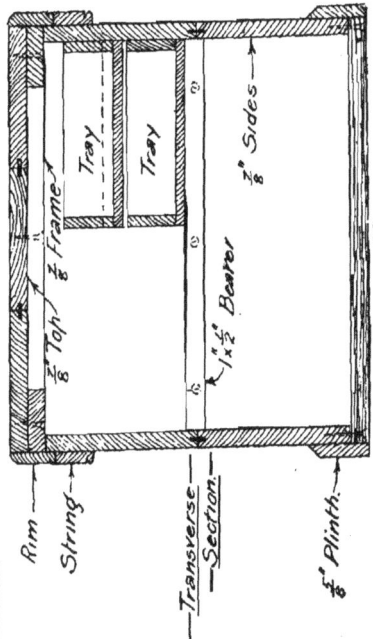

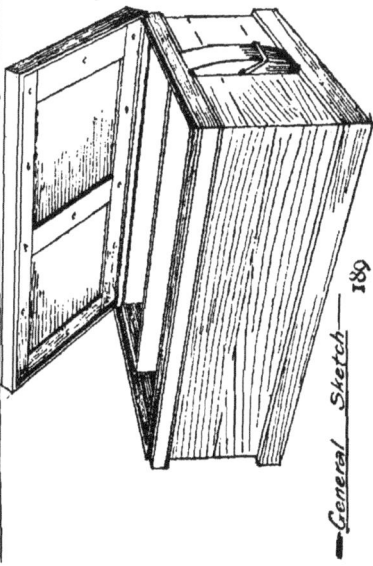

FIGS. 186 TO 189.—TOOL CHEST

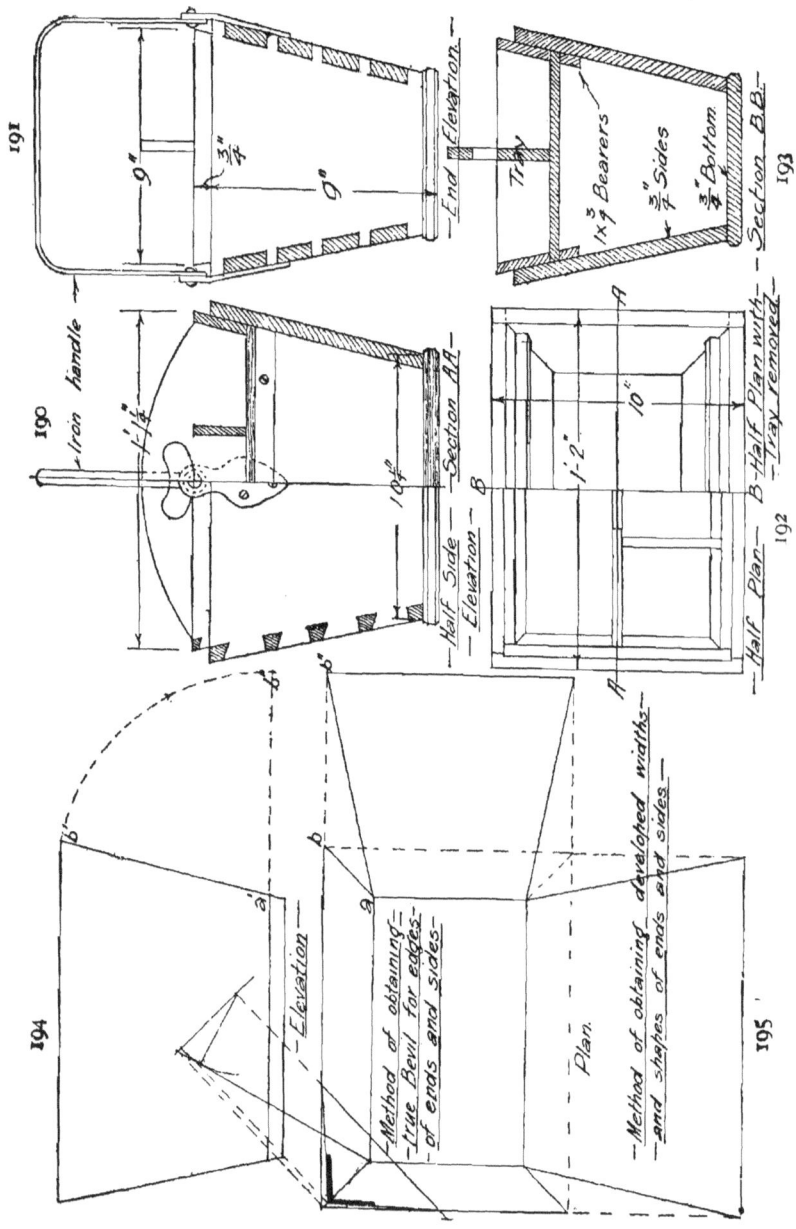

FIGS. 190 TO 195.—HOUSEMAID'S BOX.

Labels within figures:

191

9"
3/4"
9"

— End Elevation —

iron handle

190

1 1/4"

10 1/2"

Half Side
— Elevation —

— Section A.A. —

B

Tray

1 x 3/4 Bearers

3/4 Sides

3/4 Bottom

193
— Section B.B. —

A

10"

1' 2"

A

— Half Plan —   — B Half Plan with —
192   — Tray removed —

194

b
a

b
a

— Elevation —

— Method of obtaining —
— true Bevil for edges —
— of ends and sides —

— Plan. —

— Method of obtaining developed widths —
— and shapes of ends and sides —

195

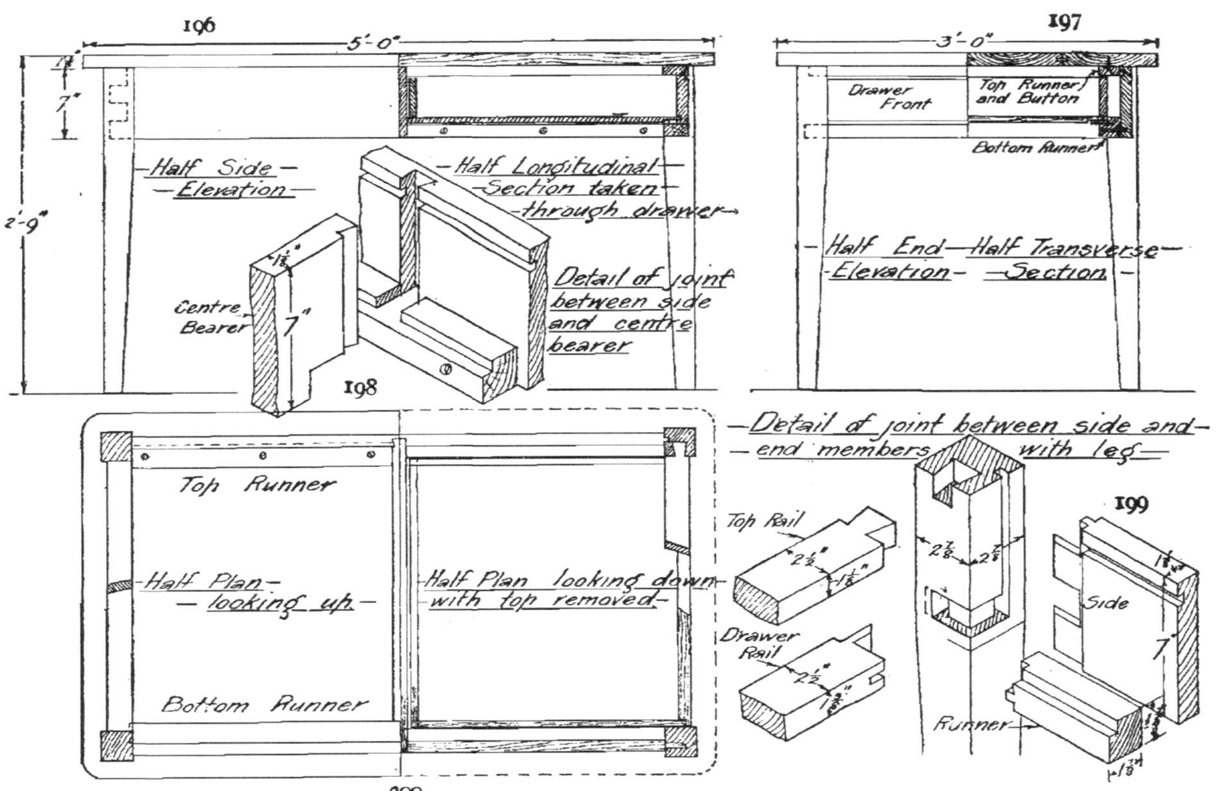
196
5'-0"
7"
2'-9"
-Half Side-
-Elevation-
-Half Longitudinal-
-Section taken-
-through drawer-
Detail of joint
between side
and centre
bearer
Centre
Bearer
7"
198
197
3'-0"
Drawer
Front
Top Runner
and Button
Bottom Runner
-Half End-Half Transverse-
-Elevation- -Section-
Top Runner
-Half Plan-
-looking up-
-Half Plan looking down-
-with top removed-
Bottom Runner
200
-Detail of joint between side and-
-end members with leg-
Top Rail
$2\frac{1}{2}$"
Drawer
Rail
$2\frac{1}{2}$"
$2\frac{7}{8}$
$2\frac{7}{8}$
199
Side
7"
Runner

FIGS. 196 TO 200.—SMALL KITCHEN TABLE.

quantities of the stuff from the drawings, making the usual allowances, the material being preferably clean white fir. Glue up the top with a tongue joint. Glue up drawer bottoms with a square joint. Take all other pieces out of winding, and shoot the face edges and reduce to the width. Set out rails of sides and ends and mortise the legs, arranging the tenons double-shouldered and mortises as shown in Fig. 199. Fit in centre bearer with the joint as shown in Fig. 200, taper the legs as indicated, removing all the stuff from the internal faces. Rebate the lower drawer runners and fit them to legs in the manner shown in Fig. 199. Groove the sides to receive the buttons for fixing the top. Glue the sides and the legs together ; screw the bottom runners on to sides, as shown in Fig. 198. Glue the drawer rails to legs; fit in centre bearer, clean up the top, shooting the edges and rounding the corners. Prepare the top runner ; place the frame in an inverted position on the underside of the table top, and insert one screw through the centre of the top drawer rail and through the centre bearer into the top. Insert the combined top runners and buttons into the grooves made in the sides to receive them, and insert screws through them into the top. This fixes the top to the sides, but allows it to shrink towards the centre. Fit the drawer fronts, prepare the sides, groove the sides and fronts to receive the bottoms, dovetail the sides, and mark the pins on the front for a lap dovetail and on the backs for an ordinary dovetail. The width of the back should be equal to the effective depth of the drawer. Dress up drawer buttons, cut to the dimensions, and bevel the edges to fit the grooves in the sides and fronts of drawers. The drawer is glued up, the bottom is slid into the grooves, and screwed upwards to the back. Clean off drawers and fit them, work a small bead on top and bottom edges of drawer fronts.

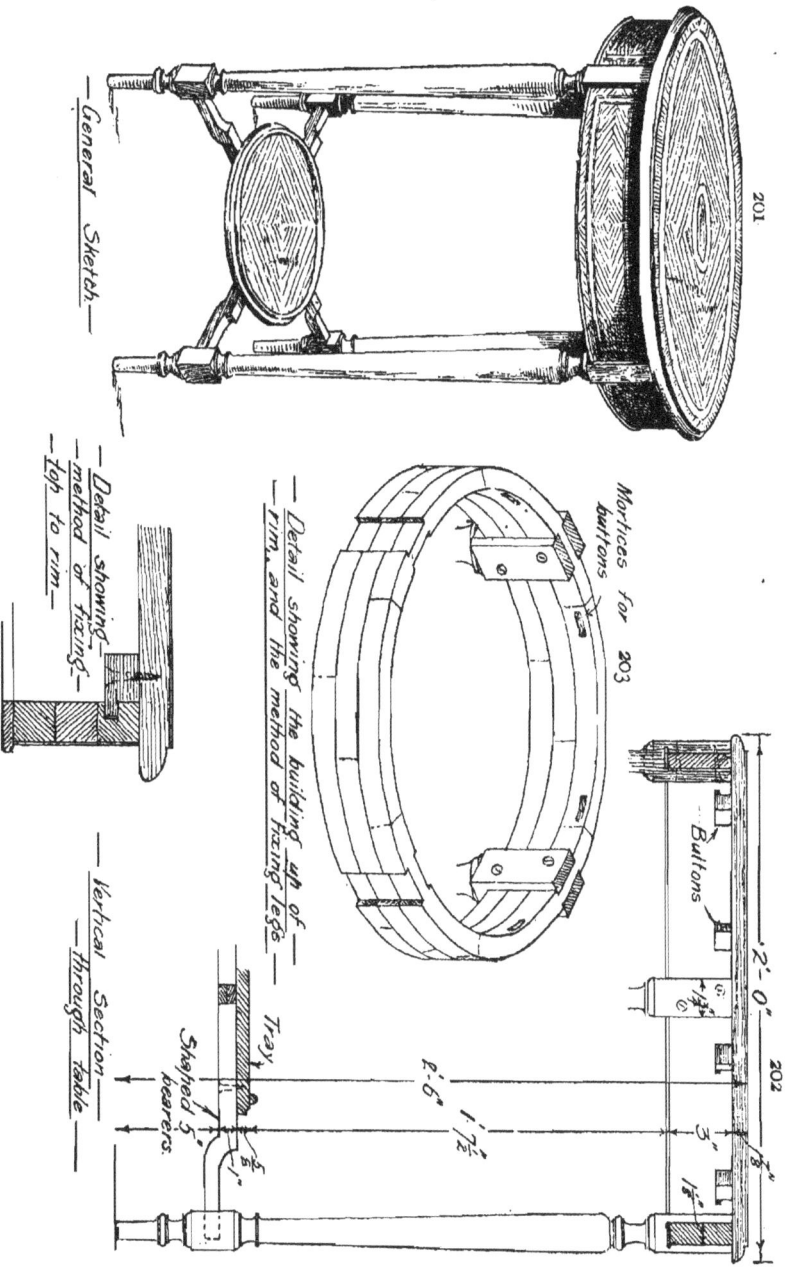

General Sketch

201

Detail showing method of fixing Top to rim

204

Mortices for 203 buttons

Detail showing the building up of rim, and the method of fixing legs

Buttons

Vertical Section through table

Tray

Shaped bearers

2' 0"

202

2' 6"

1 7½"

3"

Buttons

Occasional Table.—Take off the quantities of
the material from the drawings, shown in the
Figs. 201 to 204, making the usual allowances.
The top, the rim, and the tray should be preferably of Honduras mahogany, the legs and the
shaped bearers of Cuba mahogany. The rim is built
up as shown in Fig. 203. Strike and cut out a templet in white pine ¼ inch thick for a length equal to
one-fourth of the circumference of the rim. Mark
and cut out a series of segmental pieces in 1-inch
stuff. Build up as shown in Fig. 203 to form the
complete circular rim, dowelling the heading joints.
When this is dry, strike the outer face from a centre
with a radius rod on both top and bottom edges.
Clean off to these marks with a compass plane. Set
out the position of the legs, and cut housings as
shown. Sink eight mortises 1½ inch by ⅜ inch to
receive the buttons for fixing the top. Veneer the
rim as previously described in the article on veneering. Turn the legs or obtain legs turned, sink a
slot to form a forked joint to fit into the housings
as shown in Fig. 203. Mortise the lower square
faces to receive the shaped bearers.

Veneer the top and the tray. Cut the shaped
bearers, halve them at the centre, cut tenons at their
ends, and fit to legs. After veneering the top and
the tray, work the mouldings about their edges.
Clean up the veneered surfaces. Glue and screw the
legs to the rim and the shaped bearers. At this stage
the work should be polished. Invert the lower frame,
and fix to the underside of the top with buttons,
as shown in Figs. 202 and 204. Screw the tray to
the bearers from the underside, as shown in Fig. 202.

Prepare four segmental pieces 3/16 inch in thickness to project 3/16 inch beyond the lower edge of
the rim.

Work a bead about the outside edge and glue and
screw to the lower edge of the rim, as shown in Fig. 204.

INDEX

———

www.ingramcontent.com/pod-product-compliance
Lightning Source LLC
Chambersburg PA
CBHW021148090426
42740CB00008B/1008